The Nature Watch Collection
Collection
BOOK ONE

The Nature Watch Collection
Collection
BOOK ONE

by
GERRY RISING
with the photographs of
HAROLD STIVER

Published by William R. Parks
Stanwrite@aol.com

www.WRParks.com

To Doris and Elaine

The cover background is a section of a topographic map of southwestern New York State where much of the hiking described in these columns took place. The south central part of the map is Allegany State Park.

THE NATURE WATCH COLLECTION
BOOK ONE

For over twenty years I have been writing a weekly "Nature Watch" column for *The Buffalo News*. Originally the columns appeared on Mondays, but for many years now they have appeared in the Sunday edition. As I write in mid-2012, over 1100 columns have appeared.

I have often been asked to make these columns available in book form, but until recently I have had neither the time nor the inclination to collect and reedit the columns. Instead, I posted all of them on a website I maintained at the University at Buffalo. Recently, however, that site has had recurring problems with many of the columns lost in the process.

That problem provoked my interest in preserving these columns by some other means. When I communicated that interest to my agent, Bill Parks, he encouraged me to begin collecting them for publication.

Happily, Harold Stiver, the superb Canadian nature photographer, has agreed to join me in this project and almost all of the photographs that accompany the columns are his. Only those otherwise credited are taken by others. For those of you as yet unfamiliar with his work, you have a real treat ahead.

It is important that I note at the outset that natural history is an avocation and not a vocation for me. I spent my professional life as a mathematics teacher and have returned to a lifelong hobby of bird watching in my dotage. When the opportunity came up to take over the newspaper's natural history column back in 1992, I asked the then editor of *The Buffalo News*, Murray Light, if I couldn't restrict my writing to birds. His answer was straightforward – "No." I have come to thank him for that response as it has forced me to extend my interests in many directions. Fortunately, I have found the professional scientists to whom I have turned regularly for assistance to be forthcoming far beyond what their duties should require and an outsider should expect. I hope that I have assigned the credit they deserve in those columns to which they contributed their expertise.

Gerry Rising   June 2012

Contents

1. HUMMINGBIRDS

April 8, 1991

Ruby-throated Hummingbird

This was my first column for The Buffalo News.

Start small, they say. If so, what better topic for a first column than hummingbirds, the tiniest members of the bird world? The ruby-throated hummingbird, our only regular local species, will not arrive for another three or four weeks; but ably representing it and the other 338 members of this strictly New World family were Esther and Robert Tyrrell, who presented the annual Hayes Lecture at the Buffalo Museum of Science on April 14, 1991. Mrs. Tyrrell's talk, "Hummingbirds: Jewels of the Jungle," described the adventures of this husband-wife team in the swamps and forests of the Caribbean seeking out all sixteen species that occur there. To illustrate her talk, she showed her husband's beautiful stroboscopic photographs of these exquisite birds. Among them is the world's tiniest bird, the bee hummingbird.

Broad-billed Hummingbird

Anyone who has seen some of their color pictures in the Tyrrells' two books or in the *National Geographic* and other magazines will readily agree that they are incomparable. They follow an honorable tradition of hummingbird strobe photographs developed by Harold Edgerton of M.I.T. in the 1930s and extended as a hobby by former DuPont president Crawford Greenewalt. We all recognize Edgerton's stop-action strobe shots of golf swings and bullets smashing through light bulbs, but fewer realize that he also used this technique to freeze the 4800 wing beats per minute flight of these pennyweight birds. Greenewalt improved and Tyrrell essentially perfected this technique. The Tyrrells' long term goal was to capture on film by this means every hummingbird species.

I am especially sensitive to the difficulty of photographing hummingbirds, because as youngsters Tom Killip and I found one of their thumbnail-sized nests and tried to take pictures of the incubating female. The bird's minute size forced us to get so close that, even with flash, we never could get its body and its long bill both in focus at the same time. Clearly the Tyrrells' photographic techniques have solved such problems, but their solutions require packing 400 pounds of equipment into some of the most inhospitable environments imaginable.

Until last year my only hummingbird observations were of ruby-throats here and broad-tailed hummingbirds on visits to Colorado and Utah. (The broad-tail is the noisiest North American hummer, its tail feathers whirring as it swoops about.) But then last fall one of the west coast species appeared at a feeder — one of those red sugar water dispensers — in Grimsby, Ontario. After a long wait several of us saw this bird for a few seconds: an immature or adult female, either a rufous or an Allen's hummingbird; in this plumage it is impossible to distinguish between them in the field. Mrs. Tyrrell informed me that, although this is a quite remarkable record, her wide correspondence indicates that many hummingbird species are extending their ranges. Could this be a positive effect of global warming?

How this hummingbird could remain in Canada until early December, two months after the departure of the last ruby-throat, was also explained to me by Mrs. Tyrrell. To survive cold nights these birds fluff up their feathers to provide insulation and then lower their body temperature, thus inducing a torpor or semi-hibernation that reduces their metabolism by a factor of fifty. In this torpor hummingbirds are often thought to have died and are picked up by observers who are then astounded when their body heat "resurrects" the tiny bird.

The Tyrrells consider themselves scientific amateurs, but if they are it is in the fine tradition of Osa and Martin Johnson.

2. SAW-WHET OWL

April 15, 1991

Northern Saw-whet Owl

In a hallway of our home hangs a painting of a saw-whet owl by Guy Coheleach. It is a valued possession since its subject is one of my favorite birds. Out of the painting stares a seven-inch long, fluffed out, tawny butterball with its yellow irises almost covered by big black pupils.

But this painting in no way represents the saw-whet owl that my wife and I found hidden in a pine grove of a local nature preserve in mid-March. This bird seemed much thinner, perhaps a distant, less affluent cousin of the little fatty of the painting. To gain some sense of the size of this diminutive owl, hold up together three fingers of one hand: the bird could easily hide behind those fingers.

4

This is always a difficult bird to find. Although we had been given specific directions to a half dozen small pine trees, it took us several minutes to locate the owl. It suddenly materialized like Alice's Cheshire cat where I was certain I had looked before.

I had a similar experience several years ago cross country skiing through a thicket along Ellicott Creek near the University at Buffalo campus. Straightening up from bending under a low snag, I found myself blinked at sleepily by one of these little owls from a distance of less than three feet. It never even flushed as I awkwardly pushed on through the brush.

As this suggests, the saw-whet owl is an extremely tame little bird. We were able to approach that nature preserve owl closely before its increasing concern caused us to back away to a less threatening distance. If you ever find one of these birds — and dozens of them quietly pass through northern states across the country in March and April — I also encourage you not to disturb it. Unthreatened, it will often remain in the same area for days and even weeks. You will be well rewarded. Even my wife, who is only marginally tolerant of birds, was charmed by this Lilliputian representative of the notoriously vicious strigiform order.

Larger raptors like barred and great horned owls occasionally prey on saw-whet owls, but the smaller owls are hunters too. Their food is most often rodents and frogs; however, at this season this saw-whet almost certainly thinned the numbers of the juncos and white-throated sparrows that foraged the ground nearby. The only prey I ever observed in the talons of a saw-whet was a junco, but bigger (still only eight inch) females have been known to kill and devour red squirrels.

Saw-whet owl is a strange name. It sounds like something someone dreams up toward the end of the cocktail hour, like left tern or O'Hara cardinal or coffee chat, but there is a reason for this one. Only once have I heard the repeated metallic, whistled snee'-awww notes of the courtship song of this species. They wafted down from the midnight forest of Calamity Mountain to our Adirondack campsite at Flowed Land, and they did indeed sound like the working of a file back and forth, back and forth across the serrations of a saw. The saw-whet has another song as well, a one-note whistle repeated every second for minutes on end. Its quality is very different, yet it too could be taken for saw filing.

Although many of the saw-whet owls seen here at this time of year are migrants, some do nest in our northern states as they do in all Canadian provinces, most often in the deep, often boggy and pine covered recesses of such sanctuaries as Bergen Swamp and Allegany State Park in western New York. Evening visitors to these and other heavily wooded areas, especially in March and April, should listen for their eerie notes.

3. ALGONQUIN

April 22, 1991

Spruce Grouse

Twenty years ago Al Chestnut paddled and portaged us for eleven days through the western part of Algonquin Park in Ontario, Canada: from Kiosk partly over trailless areas across the Nipissing River, down to Smoke Lake, and then out the Oxtongue River to Huntsville. That trip was in early May just after the ice went out.

I best recall two things about that trip. I was unprepared physically and did not contribute my share. Even so I was constantly bone weary. And I was frightened. I had never been in the north in spring and I was not ready for the skim of ice on the lakes each morning reminding me what a swamped canoe would mean, the morass of the trails sucking at our boots and several times even pulling them off, or the racing river currents at each turn driving over the bank straight on into the forest and trying their best to take our heavy old canvas canoe with them.

Memories of that trip flooded back when nine of us drove to Algonquin two weeks ago looking for eight northern species — two mammals, six birds — only one of the eight occurring in western New York.

No canoeing this time: the lakes were almost all frozen solid. So too was the ground and snow cover was only a few inches, making hiking reasonably easy.

The easiest bird, common raven, we found as soon as we entered the park. From then on the "cruck" calls of these large crows were part of the background music.

Our second target was spruce grouse, a much tougher goal. Even though we had been directed by Ron Tozer, the helpful park naturalist, to a two-acre spruce grove, we searched for over an hour before Dick Collins found one.

But then we were all in for a treat. Spruce grouse are similar in size to ruffed grouse but the male is quite different in appearance. It shows much more quite beautiful black and white coloration topped by striking red eyebrows. They are remarkably fearless — some see that differently: a local name is fool hen — and this male was no exception. It strutted to within inches of us, posed for observation and photographs, and showed us its noisy wing-whirring display flight up to a nearby branch. In all the years I had spent in spruce grouse country in the Adirondacks and the Boundary Waters of Minnesota as well as in Algonquin, I had never seen one before, so this was a special thrill for me.

It took us still more time to check off boreal chickadee. Bobbie Byron finally located four in pines just west of Lake of Two Rivers. This is a shy, brown-capped chickadee whose call has a buzzier quality than the black-capped and Carolina chickadees that come to feeders of the United States.

That evening we had our first miss. Imitation wolf howls brought no response from the pack that often frequents the area. But early the next morning we did find our other mammal: three moose stared back at us from the roadside. All moose are antlerless in spring; one of these wore a radio collar instead. The previous day we had followed moose tracks and seen where they had stripped bark from red maples.

We completed our successes with a pair of gray jays. This species, also known as Canada jay and — accurately — camp robber, is a particular favorite of mine. In coloration it looks like a big chickadee; it is much quieter and slyer than our blue jay.

Despite constantly listening for their light tapping, we missed our final targets, the two species of three-toed woodpeckers. We had known that they were long shots, so we returned home well satisfied with what we had found. Our score in two days: one of the two mammals and four of the six birds.

4. HIKER'S LOG

April 29, 1991

Yellow-bellied Sapsucker

March 27. Little Valley. My first trail hike of the year. A sedentary winter lifestyle has left me in poor physical condition, so the nine miles is a serious test. My shins, calves, and finally hips keep me informed.

Three hen turkeys quietly feed on the trail. Seeing me, they shoulder each other off the path and melt into the woods.

Along a ridge are several acres of blowdown: dozens of beeches, some twenty inches in diameter, thrown about by highly localized wind gusts. The absence of overhead canopy encourages the bare raspberry branches to reach out and tear at my clothes. A fox sparrow, like a big, richly dressed and redder song sparrow, works its way through the tangle.

Rolling thunder announces not only the shower that is to come but also lightning, a threat on this exposed ridge. I welcome the start down.

On the north slope are ridges of snow but also a few bright spots of green against the drab brown forest floor. Ground pine pushes up through the leaf clutter as do two ferns: Christmas fern, with uncharacteristically broad stocking-shaped leaves alternating along its stems; and evergreen wood-fern, its lovely big green fronds quite out of keeping with the time of year.

Along the road back the earliest flower, the coltsfoot, grows in sandy margins. Several groups of these little dandelion-like yellow blossoms perch atop straight, ugly, asparagus stems.

April 2. Salamanca. Three to five inches of snow cover the ground and some of the time it snows hard. My footprints are already covered when I hike back to my car.

Near the Allegheny River are three richly colored male bluebirds. Three phoebes, widely separated, glean the forest margins for early insects. They do not call yet but characteristically wag their tails.

April 12. Red House in Allegany State Park. A beautiful clear day, the winter brown of the hillsides taking on a rosy hue from budding trees.

The long roll of a pileated woodpecker drilling breaks the forest silence.

Leeks are everywhere and a few skunk cabbages have pushed up cones in boggy swales. The Christmas ferns have replaced their leathery appearance with a healthier green. The brown leaves of the forest floor are giving way to small plants, some already in blossom. I find hundreds of what I believe to be white, lavender, and blue hepatica. A single pansy-like but tiny yellow blossom I key from my field guide: it is a round-leaved yellow violet, its minute flower on a stem separate from its two heart-shaped leaves. Patches of grass remind me of home duties to come.

Small groups of gray juncos dart off, flashing their white tail feathers. They are accompanied by the first three hermit thrushes of my birding year. Two of the juncos make high pitched squeeks that sound like those bird calls that twist metal against metal.

A winter wren tinkles its long and remarkably loud song from a hemlock grove. A male yellow-bellied sapsucker – would you call your worst enemy that name – flies smoothly after a female. These handsome woodpeckers light on a dead stub near me, the male *hoy-hoy*ing in exuberance.

A creek is newly dammed by beavers. Three common mergansers career off and miss watching me teeter across on a yellow birch log one of the beavers has conveniently felled.

It is not yet the middle of April but a few flies buzz underfoot and a bumblebee dashes by. In the leafless trees I see several old bird nests. Only one can I identify: it is the tiny lichen-covered nest of a gnatcatcher.

As the afternoon shadows lengthen and I struggle up a bank to my car, I think how in these walks I have been witnessing a vernal rebirth as esthetically attractive to me as the art of that other renaissance.

5. HAWK WATCH

May 6, 1991

Broad-winged Hawks

Just inside the east entrance of Lakeside Memorial Park in Hamburg a jogger passed a line of parked cars and a group of people sitting on lawn chairs looking up at the sky with binoculars. He slowed to a stop and asked pleasantly, "What are you folks doing?"

One of the observers responded, "We're looking at hawks."

The runner peered up briefly and, seeing nothing but blue sky and clouds, shook his head and jogged on. I am certain that he thought that he had been caught by the old "Look! Look!" trick.

But as the jogger trotted down the road into the park, I was looking at a kettle of almost 100 hawks. (Kettle is the term hawk watchers have adopted for such a group of hawks. It was chosen because the hawks appear like those tiny bubbles that move about in a seething pot just before it comes to a boil.)

Even with my binoculars the hawks were tiny specks in the sky, perhaps a half-mile overhead. Some flew in line, others in slow circles, but all moved northeast toward the eastern end of Lake Erie. There a few would swing to the west and would soon pass the hawk watching station at Grimsby; most would continue northeast and would be seen by hawk watchers at Braddock's Bay near Rochester and farther east at Oswego's Sandy Ponds lookout. They would then continue north to breed in the vast forests of the Adirondacks and Canada.

It was a quite remarkable experience to have so many hawks in one binocular field. The tiny dots appeared like those no-see-ums that circle in front of your eyes in the summer woods. After you look down to rest your neck, it is very difficult to find them again.

At this distance it took an expert like Roberta McDonald, who regularly reports the numbers of migrating raptors passing this location to the Hawk Migration Association of North America, to point out species to me. Most were broad-winged hawks, less than half the size of our resident red-tails. But soaring with the broad-wings on this late April morning were a few ospreys, those almost eagle-sized fish hawks, as well as turkey vultures, sharp-shinned hawks, and kestrels. Nearer to us two Cooper's hawks that reside in the park woods flew with graceful wing beats, courting in slow circles only part way up to the migrants.

Over time rarer birds are seen from this vantage point as well. This year, for example, both bald and golden eagles have been recorded here as have goshawks, those fierce symbols of the wild north country. Another rare hawk, the merlin, will probably be seen later.

Where we sat we could feel the wind blowing from the north off Lake Erie. This would seem to oppose this flight; instead the light breeze contributed to the lift that helped the raptors soar.

To see why, you need only recall from junior high school science three weather effects: (1) land changes temperature faster than water, (2) cold air flows toward warm, and (3) heated air rises. On this sunny spring day, the lake remained much colder than the land to its east and the air cooled by the lake flowed inland toward the air heated by the land, thus creating the breeze we felt. This onshore breeze drove a wedge under the warmer air, forcing that air upward in what are called thermals. It was this rising air that provided the lift for the migrating hawks.

In exactly the way hawks do, glider pilots utilize such thermals to maintain altitude or even to rise to higher levels. In fact glider pilots often take cues from nearby soaring hawks.

On that day there was very little wind so the birds had to fly thousands of feet above us to take advantage of the thermals. If there had been a wind out of the south of perhaps 10 to 20 miles per hour, what I have described would have taken effect at a much lower level and we would have been able to watch the birds just a few hundred feet overhead.

Even the jogger would have seen them then.

6. THE FLORIDA PANTHER

May 13, 1991

Mountain Lion
U.S. Department of Agriculture photo

The Florida panther is one of the rarest wild animals in North America. With its range now restricted to remote regions of the Everglades, this formerly widespread southeastern subspecies of the mountain lion now numbers less than 50 individuals. It is listed for protection under the federal Endangered Species Act; yet legal interpretations of this act submitted by the Solicitor's Office of the Department of the Interior will, unless modified, almost certainly push this beautiful animal and quite possibly several others over the brink into extinction.

This is a case in which I believe lawyers are disserving the natural world. Consider the story and judge for yourself.

One of the reasons why small populations are so extremely difficult to save is the fact that close inbreeding causes genetic defects. (Thus for the human species religious bans against incest serve an important biological purpose.) The small population of Florida panthers was already suffering from inbreeding when seven additional panthers were released in the Everglades. This new stock responded to the inbreeding problem, but unfortunately a few of these seven animals were individuals from a different subspecies from South America. When they successfully interbred with the Everglades population they produced two hybrid strains.

Most of us would respond, so what? We're interested in the continued presence of these animals in this remote region, not in their genetic history. It seems, however, that the legal interpretations communicated to the Fish and Wildlife Service say otherwise. The lawyers' position is that hybrids should not be protected, that in fact protecting hybrids jeopardizes a species' continuing existence.

I point out in fairness that there is sometimes a reason for this position. Suppose, for example, a northern population of some species declines and a southern strain is introduced to increase that population. The result might be that the hybrid offspring, like the southern strain, would not be able to withstand the northern weather and the entire population would be wiped out. Some say that this is exactly what happened to the bob-white in New York State.

That may be, but the result in this case could be no Florida panthers at all. Following the logic of this interpretation, all of these panthers will soon be tainted with hybrid genes and therefore no longer the designated population. Protection will be removed along with the funding necessary to guard these animals from poachers. The inevitable result: some trophy room will soon be graced by the mounted head of the last southeastern mountain lion.

In fact four other extremely rare species share the threat of this interpretation: the grey wolf, the red wolf, the northern spotted owl, and the blue whale. And as a direct result, one subspecies, the dusky seaside sparrow, has already tilted over into extinction. Note, by the way, the inclusion on that list of the spotted owl, already under attack by west coast lumbermen who wear t-shirts reading, *Save a Job: Kill an Owl.*

Will all of these species be lost to us? Not quite yet. Stephen J. O'Brien and Ernst Mayr have written in a recent issue of *Science* to urge specific legal modifications that would provide appropriate protection to these and other endangered populations. Mayr is perhaps the best known systematist in the world and his voice should have some influence. The next chapter of this story will be determined not only by the intellectual response to their article but also the political response to pressures brought by people like us.

Meanwhile the episode calls to mind Shakespeare's suggestion, "The first thing we do, let's kill all the lawyers."

7. SPRING MIGRATION

May 20, 1991

Chestnut-sided Warbler

Early one morning too many years ago Howard Miller took an eleven-year old beginning bird watcher to Highland Park in Rochester, a park internationally known for its May Lilac Festival. Before the lilac bushes bloom to attract thousands of visitors, you can usually find small numbers of interesting birds there.

But this morning was to prove quite different. The slanting rays of the early morning sun sparkled not on lilac blossoms but instead on hundreds of warblers. Every one of the lilac bushes was ornamented like the plates in a field guide by a half dozen to a dozen of these beautiful birds. Howard pointed out to the excited youngster 21 warbler species, about half of which the boy had never seen before. He could hardly record their names fast enough: palm, black-throated blue, Wilson's, cerulean, myrtle, chestnut-sided, redstart; the list went on and on. The colors were stunning: yellows, reds, and blues against intricate black and white patterns. And there were 20 to 30 of each kind.

There were other birds as well: rose-breasted grosbeaks, vireos, a brown thrasher, kinglets, thrushes, towhees, purple finches; but the warblers were center stage.

It was a wonderful experience, one I – for I was that youngster – have never matched and will never forget. But the very next day the show was over. I returned hopefully but found only a few dozen birds remaining.

What caused this spectacular brief fall-out of migrants? Serious scientists as well as bird watchers have sought the answer to this question for many years. In the April issue of *Birding* magazine, biologist Kenneth Able of the State University at Albany summarizes much of what is known about this curious phenomenon. Here is a quick summary:

Most birds migrate at night, flying in the first three hours of darkness, some moving shorter distances at low levels just before dawn. "Weather," says Able, "is the single most important factor in determining if the bird will migrate on a given night." Best conditions for spring migration are a flow of warm south or southwest wind following a high-pressure system and just ahead of a cold front. The clockwise winds around the high and the counterclockwise winds around the low combine to enhance these conditions. Such systems occur over the Niagara Frontier quite regularly in March, April, and May: on May 13th, for example, Buffalo experienced exactly these conditions.

But this is only part of the story. With these conditions large numbers of birds will simply pass through the region. What is also necessary to produce an event like the one in Highland Park is a local barrier that stops a strong migration flow. Such a local barrier could be rain, opposing northerly winds, low cloud cover, or fog. These conditions occur much less often and usually involve what weathermen call an occluded front, where a warm and cold front meet.

To a lesser extent the Great Lakes provide a migration barrier and so woodlots along the south shore of Lake Erie or Lake Ontario like those in the Tifft Nature Preserve are good spring birding spots. But the really spectacular shows require the unusual weather conditions Able describes.

Of course there is one additional requirement: you have to be there at the time all of these weather features coincide in order to take advantage of such a unique turn of events. That is the reason bird watchers pay special attention to national and local weather maps. They're looking for a combination of circumstances that occurs once or – I hope – twice in a lifetime.

8. BEGINNING BOTANISTS

May 27, 1991

Bunchberry

One thing that discourages the beginning botanist is the sheer number of plant species to be identified. Over 1600 wildflowers have been catalogued in Erie County alone. That is about five times the number of birds seen here and at least ten times the number of mammals. How can you even get started?

The best way to learn flowers is to join one of the Buffalo Museum of Science flower identification classes or one of the field trips sponsored by the museum and other organizations. Most classes are timed to the appearance of the early spring flowers called ephemeals, but the Tifft Nature Preserve 2:00 p.m. Sunday walks continue through the year. Individuals and family groups do not have to register to join these guided tours.

But it is also possible to learn at least the common flowers on your own.

Flower identification is not an expensive activity. You don't need the binoculars and telescopes of bird watchers and astronomers. What you do need, however, is a good reference book. For many years I have used the Peterson and McKenny *Field Guide to*

Wildflowers. Although I have some misgivings about this book, a quick check with more serious botanists supports this choice. I especially like the *Reader's Digest North American Wildlife*, but it is quite large to carry in the field. For those interested in other aspects of nature too, however, it makes up for its size by its coverage from mammals to mushrooms by way of birds, reptiles, fish, and flowers.

It would be nice to be able to be able to identify at a glance every wild plant, but that should not be the goal of a beginner. Instead, first learn a few species well. Keep a written record of your identification with date and location. Add two or three to your list each time you go afield and you will be surprised at how quickly your knowledge expands.

Here are some other suggestions for beginners:

Concentrate on plants when they are in flower, especially the big showy ones.

Don't spend time differentiating among quite similar flowers like violets, orchids, anemones, or daisies. On the other hand do add to your list when the species of a genus are easy to separate. A good example is the trilliums. Last month no one could have mistaken the white trillium, the provincial flower of Ontario, the painted trillium, white with purple highlights, and the purple trillium or wakerobin. (This year Bud Pearson and his wife also showed me a rare yellow form of wakerobin near their Springville home.)

Use where and when as identification tools. Just as you look for water lilies in a pond or marsh, look for goldenrods in an open field, bunchberries in the forest, and pitcher plants in a bog. Most early flowers like trout-lily and trilliums are no longer to be found, but the June flowers are ready in line to replace them.

Here is a list of distinctive flowers that a beginner might set as an initial goal for this year. These flowers are not easily confused and are still blooming or will bloom later:

Fragrant waterlily, bullhead-lily, marsh marigold, mayapple, pitcher-plant, Indian pipes, white clover, bunchberry, poison ivy, jewelweed, Queen Anne's lace, common milkweed, Dutchman's breeches, forget-me-not, common plantain, orange hawkweed, butter-and-eggs, common mullein, partridgeberry, bluets, teasel, common ragweed, coltsfoot, common burdock, common dandelion, chicory, common cattail, skunk cabbage, Jack-in-the-pulpit, Canada lily, Solomon's-seal, Canada mayflower, false Solomon's-seal, and moccasin flower.

Finally, don't be put off by the numbers. When you can identify 32 wildflowers, you may only know 2% of those in the area, but you will also be among the 2% of the human population to know this many. As you look for these flowers I predict that you will learn others as well.

9. BARN OWL

June 3, 1991

Barn Owl

WANTED! ALIVE!

Killer may be found lurking in a barn loft
or silo, appearing at dusk to wander silently
over open meadows in search of victims.
Do not approach.

If you observe this perpetrator, contact this
writer immediately!

Of course this killer is a killer of mice and rats, not people. Armed only with talons and beak, it is definitely not dangerous. It is the barn owl, a.k.a. monkey-faced owl, golden owl, and other colloquial names. Formerly rather common in this region, they are now very difficult to find here.

Local birders have searched for barn owls for years. Often when we have seen barns or silos with openings that would allow these owls access, we have asked the owners if they have such a tenant. So far, no luck. In a few cases their response has begun, "A few years ago..." or even "Last year...," but never a simple yes.

Now Charles Rosenburg, who studied barn owls in Virginia for his master's degree in zoology, has moved to this area. Chuck and his brother John have stepped up the pace of the search. I will pass on to them any information communicated to me.

As part of his study Rosenburg examined owl pellets, the masses of indigestible matter that all owls regurgitate. Occasionally he found feathers of small birds, but 80 to 100 per cent of these owls' food, he says, is meadow voles and short-tailed shrews.

The barn owl is easy to identify. It is about 18 inches in length with a wingspan of 42 inches. Seen flying from below it appears white: thus the names ghost owl and spirit owl. Its back is tawny or golden. But its most prominent feature is its heart-shaped white face, quite unlike that of any other owl — or any other bird for that matter.

It makes a wide range of sounds, most discordant. Its alarm cry is a shriek that is quite frightening when heard coming unexpectedly from the dark. Other calls include snarls, rattles, hisses, and most often clicking sounds that may serve as means of communication between individual birds.

Only rarely would other owls be seen in or near farm buildings. Barn owls nest there but elsewhere as well: in tree hollows, church steeples, water towers, and even underground in abandoned woodchuck burrows. The young are voracious eaters: a month old owlet fed nine mice was hungry again just three hours later. You can imagine from this the inroads on the local mouse population made by a family of these predators.

I once climbed to a nest high up in a huge barn in Scottsville, New York. I won't do that soon again. The smell alone nearly knocked me off the ladder. There in their own filth, hissing and snapping their bills, stood three half-grown owlets, spindle-legged and knock-kneed. Their only attractive features were their cream colored faces. They could have served as object lessons for youngsters who won't clean their rooms.

Barn owls are found on every continent except Antarctica, but we live at the northern edge of their western hemisphere range. They appear to be retreating from this area. Rosenburg's research indicates that they need to forage over 200 acres or more of open grassland, a requirement that is fulfilled throughout this region, so that cannot be the problem. We simply need more information.

Help us to learn more about these most beneficial owls by contacting me if you know of one.

10. A RARE PLANETARY DISPLAY

June 10, 1991

**From left to right: our moon, Mars (the tiny dot), Jupiter and Venus
as they appeared in the western New York sky on June 15, 1991
photo produced by Alan Friedman with Starry Nights software**

*I am including this column, because today powerful computer
software is readily available that serves as a planetarium. You can
replay asstronomical events like those of that long-ago June with
these tools. In this case you need only set such a software program
to Buffalo, NY, the date to June 15, 1991 and the time to 9:30 p.m.
EDT. Then locate the new moon with its nearby celestial objects as
Alan Friedman, president of the Buffalo Astronomical Association,
has done here. And unlike earthbound residents, you won't have to
worry about cloudy skies.*

For some weeks now the planet Venus has been the bright object
in the western sky after sunset. It shines only by reflection, but it is

still the brightest light in the entire sky. This month two other planets, Jupiter and Mars, will approach Venus very closely. Then this Saturday, June 15, the thin sliver of the new moon will join the three planets to provide a stunning spectacle in the evening sky.

To gain some idea how close these four objects will appear, hold up your thumb at arm's length. From June 15 to 19 all three of the planets could hide behind that thumb. On the 15th the moon will be only about another two thumb widths away. In scientific terms, the planets will be within 2.5° with the moon another 4° away.

Of course, the planets are not on a collision course. They remain millions of miles apart. They are merely in line with your eye, an effect called a conjunction. The apparent size and brightness of the planets and moons in our solar system is determined by their distance from us as well as their size. Thus our moon appears much larger than those planets because it is closer to us, when in reality it is only a fraction of their size.

Given a break in the weather at about 9:30 p.m. on the 15th, this spectacle will be easy to see even with the naked eye. Simply find an open area with as little ground light to the west as possible and look for the new moon. The bright object to its right will be Venus. Midway between the two will be Jupiter with Mars peeping over his shoulder.

With binoculars or with a low power telescope you could observe the three planets in the same field. Venus would appear a brilliant white, Jupiter cream colored, and Mars reddish-orange. Still closer examination would reveal Venus reflecting light only from one side like a half moon and should also disclose some of Jupiter's Galilean satellites.

Some astronomers have suggested that it was a similar conjunction of Jupiter and Mars that created the Biblical Star of Bethlehem almost 2000 years ago.

*

Ernst Both, director of the Buffalo Museum of Science, has pointed out to me that the spectacle of June 15 is only part of a continuing close encounter of planets that will extend through July. It should encourage observers, he suggests, to study the nighttime skies for the many things to be seen without a telescope.

To help you to follow up Dr. Both's suggestion, I simulated on my computer the planetary positions for June and July. They do indeed provide a continuing series of interesting events. I urge you to see them for yourselves.

On the 17th the moon will be gone but the three planets will be most tightly grouped. They will appear as a triangle with sides between 1° and 2° of your 360° vision. (A degree is the width of a pencil held at arm's length.) Off to their right will be Pollux and Castor, the twin stars of the constellation Gemini.

Watch on successive nights for the planets to exchange places in line. Close encounters will occur on June 14, 17, and 23, and July 10 and 14.

Late in June you will begin to see a fourth planet, Mercury, farther to the north near the horizon, but in line with the others. As Mercury nears the other three planets early in July, the star Regulus of the constellation Leo will approach them from the opposite direction, both soon joining the parade in the evening sky. On July 13 our moon will reappear and all six will be nearly in line within 17°. From south to north they will be Venus, Regulus, Mars, the moon, Jupiter, and Mercury.

Finally in late July they will all pass below the horizon too early to be visible and this spectacular planetary show will be over.

11. BIG JANUARY

June 17, 1991

Merlin

To bird watchers competition takes the form of listing. Most active birders I know keep life lists of species identified; many go on to keep year and month lists, as well as May "big day" lists. They also keep local lists, state lists, some even world lists. And they compare with each other. "How many species have you seen so far this year?" "How many did you get yesterday?" are common inquiries.

I am not foreign to this competition. Without looking it up I can tell you that my year high in the Buffalo area was 248 species in 1988 when I tied Mike Galas. The next year he did better.

Notice that only part of that competition is with others. Much of it is with oneself. Perhaps a dozen local birders have seen more species than I have in a year, but that does not take away from my annual effort to reach 250: to improve, as that movie title has it, my personal best. To a newcomer to birding the goal of reaching a 100 species life list holds the same excitement.

Some bird watchers disdain listing as frivolous. On the other hand some of the most respected ornithologists – Ludlow Griscom, James Fisher, Roger Tory Peterson, for example – have maintained such lists.

Like the 3:45 mile and the 20-foot pole vault, there are benchmark numbers that listers try to meet or break. One of those local marks is 100 species in January. In 1989 Dick Collins, Mike Galas, and I just made it to that total, a recent record.

But this year Willy D'Anna shattered that record by seeing 105 in January, a spectacular total – something like adding a foot to the high jump mark.

In an article in *The Prothonotary*, the journal of the Buffalo Ornithological Society, D'Anna describes his achievement as a product of luck, assistance from friends who called his attention to hard-to-find species, and the mild winter. I would add to that modest assessment, his excellent skills, persistence, and many long and exhausting days in the field.

To achieve a high total in January you must see almost all the birds that are usually found in the region at that time of year. Then you must find a good number of additional unexpected species, birds seen here at other times of the year but rarely in winter.

Some unexpected species D'Anna found were: tundra swan, snow goose, ruddy duck, ring-necked duck, common black-headed gull, black-legged kittiwake, Forster's tern, yellow-bellied sapsucker, and rufous-sided towhee.

In mid-January D'Anna found his 99th species on the Statler Building in downtown Buffalo. It was a peregrine falcon, one of those rare predators that teetered on the brink of extinction when DDT still worked its insidious effects up through the food chain. Its numbers replenished through a process called hacking, it is still a very rare bird.

Then on January 18, he counted 100, again in the city. Quite remarkably it was another rare falcon: a merlin. Ellen Schopp helped him locate it in a pine grove on the University at Buffalo Main Street campus.

After that, he says, everything was anticlimactic.

Like an outstanding achievement in sports, D'Anna's record will spur others to set their sights high. And this competition will add to our ornithological knowledge of the Niagara Frontier through the more intensive fieldwork demanded. One factor that will encourage competitors is the complete absence of winter finches from D'Anna's list. In a year when they were in the region he could have added another six species!

Of course you always miss at least one bird you count on. D'Anna's nemesis was cedar waxwing.

[Added note: D'Anna's record has been surpassed several times over the years since he established it, often by young birders who seem able to spend limitless time in the field.]

12. BEAVER

June 24, 1991

Beaver Dam at Dusk

The beaver is one of those animals that has enjoyed great press. In cartoons it is usually portrayed as cute, its two big incisors giving it an ingratiating smile. When disturbed, the warning slap of its tail as it dives provides a startling and attractive signature. It is known for its lodge and dam building industry. And the dams it constructs are quite remarkable feats of engineering. I have walked along several that were 20 to 50 yards long and 8 to 10 feet high.

But the beaver is not one of my favorite animals.

My attitude is not unusual. It almost certainly reflects that of every canoe traveler from the time of the earliest Amerinds.

Imagine yourself with me in a heavily laden canoe as we round a bend in an open, smoothly flowing stream or river. We are immediately confronted by a line of loosely entangled branches and mud usually between 2 inches and 2 feet high that completely spans the stream and effectively blocks our way.

Our first thought is, "Can we ram through it?" The answer to that question depends at least as much on the ownership of the canoe as it does on the height of the dam. If we hang up like a seesaw half way across the dam, the weight in the ends of the canoe can seriously damage its midsection.

So usually if we are going downstream, we will run the bow 2 or 3 feet up onto the dam. We then have to scramble out onto this rickety structure on opposite sides of our boat, the stern paddler clambering over the packs and each of us invariably filling at least one boot with water. If the load is still quite heavy, some packs must also be removed and balanced precariously while we slide the canoe over the dam and awkwardly re-embark.

Going upstream it can be even more complicated.

We regain control of our canoe and look ahead. There a few yards away is another dam. Over it we can see a third.

By now "busy as a beaver" has taken on a very negative connotation.

I have another less selfish beef against the beaver. From my canoe in a Canadian lake I once saw about a hundred birch trees, all freshly felled by beavers, their eight-inch diameter white trunks scattered over a hillside like toothpicks. It was distressing to see these beautiful trees industriously brought down in one season, their foliage far more food than any colony of beavers could eat. It seemed an act of wanton desecration, like the time every single window was broken in my uncle's greenhouse by two eight-year-olds. Like those foolish children, the beavers once started simply could not stop.

I have, of course, been far too hard on this most attractive wild animal, which remains to me one of the central symbols of wilderness. In the 1700s widely distributed across this country, its heavy lustrous fur almost did it in. It was virtually extirpated from its continent-spanning former haunts by trapping. Its European cousin is in fact extinct in Great Britain and Scandinavia. Fortunately protective measures and changing fashions for both women and men — its fur was used in the old "stovepipe" top hats — have saved our North American beaver, but it remains an uncommon resident across much of the United States and Canada.

13. APPALACHIA

July 1, 1991

Mountain Laurel

photo by Sylvia W. Forward

Across the northern belt of states and provinces of North America "Leave the June woods to fly fishermen" is a rule to be broken at great peril. A year ago my hiking companion, Duke Colborn of Amelia Island, Florida, and I challenged that adage by hiking a section of New York's Adirondack Northville-Placid trail in June.

We lost.

Despite use of what seemed gallons of bug dope, we were continuously punished by a nightmare of no-see-ums and mosquitoes and flies and it seemed every other insect known or unknown to science. It was not a pleasant experience.

So this year we shifted our itinerary to the south. We spent seven days in early June hiking the Appalachian Trail along the North Carolina-Tennessee border between Spivey Gap and the village of Elk Park. Sections of the trail were festooned with spider webs from which dewdrops glistened each morning in the sun. Insects on the other hand were conspicuous by their absence. I don't think that I saw a dozen bugs in seven days of hiking.

This is a beautiful section of the trail and it is far enough north of the Smokies to be very little used. On only two days did we meet another soul. The dozens of through hikers, those who set out from Georgia to walk the entire 2100 miles to Maine, had passed here several weeks earlier.

My original photo is lost and this is a neighbor's rhododendron. I invite you to imagine the appearance of that Appalachian hillside covered with flowers like these. GR photo

Most of the early rhododendron blossoms were past their prime. At higher elevations, however, their season is retarded and one meadow near the 6285-foot peak of Roan Mountain was flooded with their light lavender blossoms. (For non-hikers, I note that this peak may be reached by car.) What some of the locals describe as the real show, the giant rhododendrons, would come later. They were still only budding, but the mountain laurels and the flame azaleas were in full bloom.

Flame azaleas make a striking sight. We usually found their tumbles of brilliant lily-like orange blossoms set off against the subdued greens and browns of the mature forest. Their name is perfect for they are like bright flames in the darker woods. Sometimes we could see four or five of these smokeless bonfires scattered across the steep hillsides below us.

I used to think that nothing could compare with the dogwood blossoms of southern Connecticut, but the beautiful flower clusters of the mountain laurel have easily displaced them in my personal wildflower pantheon. I have not seen this shrub growing wild in my home area of Buffalo, New York. Like the dogwood, the range of the mountain laurel is mostly south of us. The closest we come to its beauty is in our early spring fruit trees.

Picture the mountain laurel with me. Set against its waxy green leaves are a profusion of delicate pinkish-white blossoms, dozens bunched tightly into large slightly pastel snowballs. Come closer and you find that a single blossom is an inch wide pentagram, each of its five overlapping petals marked with two tiny purple dots. Near the center a thin wavy purple line is embroidered echoing the shape of the flower.

It is hard to believe that this beautiful shrub has two close relatives, bog laurel and the appropriately named lambkill, each of which is poisonous to livestock.

The rich flower array that must have covered the forest floor here in earlier spring was gone, its sunlight now cut off by the overhead canopy of 60 to 100 foot beeches, maples, tuliptrees, and oaks. Quite unlike the showy rhododendrons and laurels, the flowers that remained were most often quite tiny. Among them were clintonia, purple fringed orchis, galax, and fly-poison.

But at the edge of one of the high meadows, called "balds," we did find a rare and local Gray's lily, like the reddish-orange form of our Canada lily but more bell-shaped.

In June I much prefer the botany of the southern Appalachians to the entomology of the Adirondacks.

14. FLINT CREEK

July 15, 1991

White-eyed Vireo

Hartselle, Alabama. For two hours I walk along Flint Creek near my in-laws' home. The dense woods are lush from the almost constant rains that are this year punishing southern farmers after several years of drought.

Tufted titmice greet me as I make my way down to this 50 foot wide stream that is locally more often called a branch. My wife says that here a creek is usually a much larger stream. A river is, of course, the commanding half mile wide Tennessee just to the north.

An Acadian flycatcher calls from a tree overhanging the water. Its song is accurately described as the sound of a squeeze toy. Imagine pinching one of those child's rubber balls whose metal plug gives it an in-out sound something like [zeet'-sigh]. It is a drab little olive-gray bird that is quite uncommon in Buffalo and very difficult to separate, except by this distinctive song, from several other small insect hawkers.

Nearby but well hidden, a yellow-billed cuckoo repeats its soft, slow-paced cucking calls.

The going is very difficult. The stream has been out of its banks recently and the red clay underfoot is slimy. Walking here is like sliding on greased ice. I inch forward, grasping at trees and bushes for support. But this too poses problems. Every other bush has big thorns and nettles are ubiquitous.

A white-eyed vireo, also rare in Buffalo, responds to my spishing, its white eye accented by yellow "eye-glasses," eye rings that are connected by a band to the bird's bill. The yellow-throated vireo shares these spectacles, but not the white eye, and its song is very different. This bird sings an explosive, [chick pea', do you want to pick]. The abrupt quality of the song is reminiscent of the Canada Warbler.

Now two birds whose songs I have trouble differentiating sing alternately, almost in contrast. They are two skulkers, easy to hear, tough to see: Carolina wren and Kentucky warbler. In more open areas here the identification problem is further complicated by mockingbird imitations.

I locate the handsome warbler in the understory and now find its song easily distinguishable, but of course I will forget this distinction by the time I next hear this elusive bird in Buffalo.

My wife and mother-in-law insist that this stream, now so muddy from flooding, is the home of many water snakes. Whenever I set out for this walk, as I do each time we visit, they warn me about the poisonous water moccasin or cottonmouth. Their strictures suggest a serpent that crocodile-like might come after me on the creek bank and drag me down to the depths.

But my wife also tells me of seeing one as a child from a swimming hole, the water emptying temporarily as the snake drifted by with the current, its open mouth with its cotton-white interior easily identifying it by name.

Of course the story contradicts the warning. The children clearly went back to swimming so the threat could not be all that great.

What part of the many snake stories I am told here are true and what part the exaggerations of idle gossip is difficult to tell. I am convinced, however, that over time episodes heard second-hand are reassigned to the teller, giving authenticity to such stories as link snakes that re-combine after having been chopped into pieces or threatened hoop snakes that bite their own tails to form loops that roll away.

Sadly I am once again disappointed. I find no snakes along Flint Creek.

But later when I am cutting my in-laws' lawn I find a big ribbon snake. I hustle it off into the adjacent field so that it won't suffer the fate of all reptiles found in this yard. It is clear to me that my wife and mother-in-law, two otherwise quite gentle women, pose much more danger to snakes than those maligned creatures do to them.

15. DOG DAYS

July 22, 1991

Raccoon

The dog days of summer are upon us.

That phrase "dog days" has several connotations. At this time of year the dog star Sirius, our second brightest star, is in rather close alignment with the sun. The Romans thought that this contributed to the midsummer heat.

But it is a second interpretation that I consider here: in the South dog days are more often associated with mad dogs: that is, dogs affected with rabies. Recall the scene in both the novel and film *To Kill a Mockingbird*, when Scout's father is called upon to shoot the rabid dog as it staggers into town.

Rabies must be taken seriously. If transmitted to a human — usually through an animal bite — and untreated, it is uniformly fatal. The tissue of the brain is attacked and death is often accompanied by violent convulsive seizures. Another advanced symptom, extremely painful contraction of throat muscles when attempting to swallow, often leads the infected person to fear the sight of water. For this reason rabies has, since the time of Aristotle, also been called hydrophobia.

In the southern states rabies has always been widespread and Southerners have learned to live with the minor threat of this disease. Until recently it has been rare here in New York, but now rabid animals are found regularly, especially in counties bordering Pennsylvania, and the disease continues to spread. A few weeks ago a Hinsdale child was bitten by a rabid bat. (She was successfully treated.) Statewide in the first five months of a recent year more infected animals, 288 of them, were identified than in any earlier time period. Thus we need to be aware of this threat and to seek treatment immediately if any possibility of infection exists.

At the same time we should not become so paranoid that we no longer enjoy the out-of-doors.

With dogs now regularly inoculated against this virus, they are rarely carriers. The disease vectors now are almost always wild animals. In 1990, for example, the rabid animals identified in this state were 84 raccoons, 84 bats, 34 foxes, 23 skunks, 14 cattle, 2 dogs and 1 cat. Rabies among rodents is extremely rare, but any warm blooded animal can be infected. In Alabama my wife's great aunt died from rabies contracted from the bite of a pig she was feeding.

Threatening as it is, rabies is easy to avoid. Conservation Departments recommend that we all have pets inoculated and in control, stay away from strange pets, and most important, keep a safe distance from all wild animals.

It is especially important that parents communicate these rules to children. In the early stages rabid animals appear tame and healthy and are often easily approached, but their illness can turn them aggressive at any moment. Sicker animals are almost blind, have little motor control, and thus are easily avoided. At all times the rule is simply: Keep your distance!

There is another reason for not handling a wild animal that may be just as compelling to any caring person. If you contact a potentially rabid animal — and that's most of them — public health law requires that it be killed in order to be tested for the rabies virus. So your warm-hearted overtures may instead serve as a death penalty for a possibly healthy creature. The conservation slogan applies: "If you care leave them there."

Just over 100 years ago Louis Pasteur developed the vaccine against rabies and then applied a modification of this vaccine as a treatment for already infected patients. His treatment of an infected peasant boy is one of the great success stories of medicine. This treatment involved a series of up to 21 injections in the wall of the stomach. Fortunately this painful regimen has now been replaced by five vaccine injections in the arm. It remains, however, very important that this series of shots be started immediately after exposure to the disease.

Don't let this easily avoidable and reasonably treated disease keep you out away from the woods and fields. Just be aware of the limited danger and take reasonable precautions.

16. MUTED SPRING

July 29, 1991

Cape May Warbler

Several weeks ago one of my university colleagues, Jim Bunn, caught me before a committee meeting to comment, "Isn't it wonderful to see so many birds this spring?" Taken aback by this contradiction of my own experience but unprepared to respond, I stammered something unintelligible before the gavel deflected our attention.

Having just studied Morgan Jones' completed report of the Buffalo Ornithological Society May Bird Count, I now have some data that runs counter to Jim's experience.

Before turning to that data, I note that this count and similar ones in January, April, and October have been conducted annually by this society since the 1930s, providing a remarkable compilation, to my best knowledge unequalled on this continent. The census area includes all of western New York to a jagged north-south line through Albion, Batavia, and Warsaw, then in the southern tier reaching farther east to include Alfred and Andover. It also includes a bite of Canada extending all the way to Grimsby. This year 242 bird watchers took the field on May 19th.

The Count totals raise serious concerns. Of the 195 species recorded 49 set or tie lowest counts for the decade 1982-1991. For many of these species it is necessary to look back to the early 1960s when coverage was less intensive to find lower counts. Even with this reservation, 3 species — horned lark, Cape May warbler, and black-and-white warbler — established lows for the full 55 years.

Most critical is the fact that 14 of the decade lows are for warblers, many of them species that winter in the ever diminishing rain forests of Central and South America. The other 12 warblers with low counts are: Tennessee warbler, Nashville warbler, northern parula, yellow warbler, chestnut-sided warbler, black-throated blue warbler, yellow-rumped warbler, black-throated green warbler, blackburnian warbler, palm warbler, bay-breasted warbler, and ovenbird. In fact three-fourths of the low counts are for the so-called perching birds. Such birds as waterfowl, hawks, and owls are in much better shape.

Another way of looking at this data is by families. In addition to warblers, woodpeckers, swallows, thrushes, native sparrows, blackbirds, and finches are all down from the average counts of earlier decades.

My own experience in recent years runs parallel to this. I have been finding the same number of species in this region, but the number of individuals of all but the most common species has been very small. On May 12th, for example, a field trip to Williamsville Glen turned up 22 warbler species, high for the year. But only two species — yellow-rumped warbler and magnolia warbler — had counts of over 7 birds. The other 20 were represented by only 63 birds, an average of about 3 each. There were only 4 of the usually abundant yellow warblers.

Notice that, unlike many other warblers, most of those yellow-rumps winter in the southern United States, not in the tropics.

The evidence looks bad, but there are mitigating factors. This spring was one of the earliest of recent years: trees were fully leafed out a week to ten days ahead of schedule. The mild winter and especially warm and moist April led to a botanical bonanza. This lush growth provided a very attractive spring for wildflower and tree enthusiasts, but it made things very difficult for bird watchers. To paraphrase an old saying, you could not see the birds for the leaves.

And the delightful weather rushed the birds through the region, hell bent for their northern breeding grounds. Terry Moser of Fredonia described this phenomenon as an "over the top" migration.

I hope that these factors were responsible for these distressing counts and I hope too that next year's count will provide more encouraging data. But for now I am very disturbed about what Steve Eaton called "the most birdless spring since 1950" when he first arrived in Cattaraugus County.

17. CAMPING

August 5, 1991

Bob and Anne Bugenstein in the BWCI.
GR photo

This week four of us returned from a week in the Minnesota Boundary Waters Canoe Area (BWCI) and once again I was struck by the first question most people asked when they learned where we had been. They didn't ask, "Did you catch many fish?" (No, but then only Wally fishes and not often at that.) They didn't ask, "Did you see any large animals?" (We didn't. One reason: the moose herd has been decimated by a tick that causes them to rub off much of their protective coat. They then cannot withstand winter conditions.) They didn't ask, "How was the weather?" (Some thunderstorms, high winds, and even unusual heat, but mostly excellent.) And they didn't ask, "Were there many birds?" (There weren't.)

Instead they asked, "Was it crowded?"

Crowding is today an inevitable concern. We see newspaper and television pictures of long lines of cars standing in traffic jams at our national parks. We hear of camping reservations for the full year all taken up on the first business day in January. And some of us — me included — have had to park overnight with our families at campsite entrances hoping that a site would come open the next morning.

But the answer to the question is simply no, it was not crowded. In the 7 days we were out, we saw perhaps 40 people. Even that number was more than usual, but we were canoeing over a popular route to and along the Kiwishiwi River. Other years following less favored routes we have seen as few as a dozen people. On at least one night this year we were the only group camping on a lake with four open campsites.

How can this be? As a nation we can hardly contain our burgeoning population: we are bursting at the seams. Camping and the out-of-doors are at a peak of popularity. Improved highways and underpriced gasoline make access easier and easier. And yet paddling the length of a single lake and walking a single portage transports us to another quieter world.

I first considered this question when in the 1960s I climbed Slide Mountain in the Catskills. I spent 36 hours alone in the woods, meeting only one other person, by remarkable chance a former student. Here I was in mid-August about 80 miles, an hour and a half drive, from the largest city in the world hiking in solitude.

The answer lies in what a friend calls the tenement camping ethic: you acquire the largest tent, trailer, or RV possible with every comfort of home. You drive to a campsite where you park in line with thousands of others. And then you entertain yourselves by watching your or your neighbor's portable TV, only occasionally breaking away to drive the local roads, visit the amusement parks of the area, or attend ranger sponsored evening entertainment for crowds of hundreds. Until recently when the practice was stopped, one of these programs involved waiting in your car in a local garbage dump until a few pathetically conditioned bears came out and rooted around in the debris.

Don Nelson, a Rochester friend who hunted from a remote camp in the Adirondacks, described a similar effect: "When you get beyond the illegal hunting distance from the highways, you no longer see any hunters."

Please understand that I am not opposed to this roadside camping. Quite the contrary, I am delighted that so many are satisfied with so little. It keeps 95% of these crowded parks peaceful and serene: the woodland trails and the lakes that do not permit motors quiet and unlittered, the wildlife undisturbed, the wildflowers untrampled.

18. WIND BIRDS

August 12, 1991

Willets

Peter Matthiessen calls them wind birds.

They are less imaginatively termed shorebirds: plover and sandpiper, snipe and woodcock, yellowlegs and willet, curlew and godwit, whimbrel and phalarope. And they are already making their way south through the Niagara Frontier where I live from their breeding grounds in northern Canada. Some, like the tiny sanderling, will fly on to the remotest fringes of South America.

I am reminded of this name and of Matthiessen's beautiful essays as I stand with Mike Galas and Bill Watson watching a small flock of these birds. For a few moments they move about, each to its own concerns, along the Lake Erie edge. A lesser yellowlegs wades belly deep in the water and occasionally darts a bill at a minnow, semi-palmated and pectoral sandpipers with sanderlings search the rocks and probe the sand for insects, killdeers stand silent, one with its head tucked into its back feathers, and smaller semi-palmated plovers like obstreperous children dash about among the others.

But suddenly a wind gust picks up most of the birds and at first blown like leaves they quickly become a synchronized team. They wheel with the wind along the shoreline, flash in unison dark backs, light bellies. Their sharp falcon wings power delicate bodies in perfect formation out over the lake a few feet above the water, first one way then another until, with hardly a minute passed, they return, veer upwind now on drooping wings to touch down gently a few feet from where they rose.

Where we watch these beautiful birds, we stand on what Bill tells me is the Edgecliff member of the Onondaga limestone. This is the shelf rock northern shoreline that juts out into Lake Erie at Rock Point Provincial Park about 50 miles west of the Peace Bridge that crosses into Canada from Buffalo, New York. It is clear and sunny with temperature in the mid-70s, another of those days that Niagara Frontier dwellers who have never lived elsewhere too easily forget.

Embedded in the rock are the remaining evidence of rugose and tabulate corals left here when this was an ocean bottom over 350 million years ago. There are also deposits of silica-laden chert, still harder rock that Indians chipped and flaked into arrowheads. On the rocks windrows of the tiny shells of zebra mussels remind us of their aggressive immigration.

Between us and the sand dunes are extensive stands of the handsome purple loosestrife, another dangerous alien, this one choking out native rushes. But near them, seemingly growing out of the solid rock, are the ground-hugging red tentacles of silverweed bearing small green fronds and an occasional tiny yellow blossom.

A few butterflies visit these flowers: a monarch, cabbage butterflies — white with black dots in each wing — and a delicate little blue butterfly, I assume a spring azure.

As I focus my telescope on the shorebirds, I notice that the rough rock face is peppered with thousands of flying insects. As the sandpipers walk among them, the flies retreat, leaving bare a 6-inch radius circle around each bird. Despite this retreat, an occasional thrust picks up a laggard fly.

Bill finally separates a least sandpiper from the more numerous semipalmated sandpipers. I recall color differences between these two species by a mnemonic: the number of letters in SEMI with its

GRAY back and DARK legs, the number of letters in LEAST with BROWN back and legs GREEN or, cheating a little, YELLOW with one L.

These sparrow-sized sandpipers of the genus Calidris are more commonly known among birdwatchers as "peeps." We look for their rarer cousins, western, white-rumped, and Baird's sandpipers, without success.

But now the wind birds rise again. Over the days ahead they will drift east along the beaches to Jaeger Rocks at the eastern end of Lake Erie. From there their powerful instinctual drive will join our northwest gusts to urge them on ever south.

19. LADY BIRD JOHNSON:
MAKING THE UNITED STATES BEAUTIFUL

August 19, 1991

Lady Bird Johnson with her husband,

President Lyndon Baines Johnson

Dear Lady Bird Johnson,

I write to thank you for your lovely book, *Wildflowers across America*, and to thank you as well for your major contributions to the beautification of this country.

With only a few exceptions I have regularly regarded our United States presidents' wives with affection and respect. In your case that regard has been heightened by your interest, which I share, in the natural world.

But there is a difference between us. You have done something about it.

"The Constitution of the United States," you write, "does not mention the First Lady. She is elected by one man only. The statute books assign her no duties; and yet, when she gets the job, a podium is there if she cares to use it. I did. The public nature of the White House allowed me to focus attention on the environment, especially on plantings for roadsides and parks."

Like most others I knew before I read this book only about your sponsoring highway legislation eliminating billboards and screening automobile junkyards. That work brought to mind an essay I read years ago by Kenneth Roberts. Titled "Roads of Rememberance," the essay set against stories of the deeds of Revolutionary War heroes descriptions of the highways established in their memory, each road desecrated by a terrible proliferation of advertising signs. Where soldiers marched and fell, we read only of Burma Shave. That essay struck a chord, so I have always given full support to your efforts to address this problem.

Sadly, I note that those billboard regulations are slowly being compromised by aggressive advertisers who are unchecked by the agencies responsible for their control. Here we see from our New York State Thruway ever increasing numbers of motel advertisements, and when I drive south on interstates I find still more signs. Outside Decatur, Alabama on I-65 there is even a huge billboard advertising the Huntsville Space Center — a case of the Federal government compromising its own regulations.

Your *Wildflowers across America* is more than a coffee table book. In addition to its hundred pages of striking wildflower photographs, it also balances more technical essays by Carlton Lees with your own personal memoires. I especially enjoyed one of Lees' chapters — What is a Wildflower? — in which he exposes the weak boundaries between wildflowers and weeds, separates native plants from exotics, describes how plants evolve and "migrate," and discusses problems related to the introduction of plant species.

I knew of the difficulties associated with that attractive exotic, purple loosestrife, which we see in such prolific evidence along our roadsides just now. I was unaware, however, of the similar problems with a favorite shrub, multiflora rose. Widely used in the 1930s for hedgerows, it soon began to choke out other plants, take over open fields, and spread rapidly to new areas. I have had to rethink my attitude now that I find it grouped with that aggressive monster, kudzu.

I also appreciated Lees' word portraits of many of this country's early naturalist-explorers, among them Catesby, Bartram, Nuttall, and of course Lewis and Clark, each narrative accompanied by exquisite botanical watercolors.

Your own essays then bring into clear focus contemporary problems and show us some of your own solutions.

The Observation Tower at the Lady Bird Johnson Wildflower Center

This tower also serves as a cistern to provide water for plantings

Photo courtesy of the Center

Recently a Minnesota friend extolled the Midwest Regional Office of the National Wildflower Research Center at Chanhassen. Now I learn from this book of your own personal gifts of land, seed money, and support to establish in 1982 the original Center in Austin, Texas, in order to continue and expand your beautification programs.

This Center facilitates research on the preservation and restoration of native plants, derives from that research vital and reliable information to promote their use and conservation, and disseminates that information to governmental agencies and the public. A rapidly growing membership, now over 15,000, represents a good evaluation of this work.

Mrs. Johnson, you have indeed used your bully pulpit to advantage. I salute you for your leadership and I look forward to your continuing contributions over many years ahead.

Mrs. Johnson wrote a personal thank you note in response to this column. She died on July 11, 2007. The research center in Austin has now been renamed the Lady Bird Johnson Wildflower Center. Located at 4801 La Crosse Avenue in Austin the Center is open to visitors during Wildflower Days, March 12 to May 31 from 9:00 a.m. until 5:30 p.m.

20. ROUTE 20

August 26, 1991

A Road Sign along Route 20 near Cardiff, New York

GR photo

It is like turning back the calendar 50 years.

I am driving across New York State on Route 20. Two days ago I followed the Thruway east to Albany and I decided to compare it with this parallel older highway a few miles to the south. This is the route my family followed before the toll road was built in the 1950s.

I am pleasantly surprised.

The 300 mile trip takes less than an hour longer. Midweek traffic is light and except in towns I am able to drive at the same 55 mph speed limit.

But the opportunity to observe is very different. Here there is not the Thruway's uniform buffer zone. The farm homes are close to the road with the open country just beyond. Across much of the route nature comes to the road edge and even out onto the median. Less often mown, the grass verges are overgrown with colorful weeds.

I am proud of our neighbors who live along this highway. Their yards are well tended, their late summer gardens colorful. Demonstrating that strong heartland regard for country are the neatly displayed American flags, but I see only one of the more transient yellow ribbons.

The 50 to 100 year old homes, cobblestones often identifying this age, are well cared for. On the lawn of the single dilapidated exception is a line of ceramic ducks, clearly an effort of a housewife to counter her conditions. A number of mailboxes are ornamented with petunias or other garden flowers.

The trip is easily divided into thirds: the more urban Finger Lakes region separating the rural eastern and western sections. Although there are some attractive old homes in the middle third, it does not live up to the others. Only here do billboards intrude; only here are the excesses of a Niagara Falls Boulevard. As if in punishment, this year's drought has hit this midsection hardest. To the west and east field corn is tall and well eared; here it is less healthy, in a few cases completely lost.

Woods and fields along the route express the summer's surplus of sun rather than its water deficiency. Trees are lush and rich green, only an occasional maple showing too early a few fronds of autumnal reds and yellows. About half of the rural area is second growth forest. This part of the state seems to be returning from farms with scattered woodlots to scattered fields in the woods.

An even partial inventory of the wildflowers is lengthy. Dominant species are Queen Anne's lace, goldenrod, and ragweed with purple loosestrife forcing its way into the picture more and more as I drive west. But there is also chicory and milkweed, low bright yellow clusters of birdfoot trefoil and butter-and-eggs, taller daisies, sow-thistles, and knapweed, and in the few damp spots cattails and rushes. The deep brown burnt-out but not unattractive tassels of dock dot the fields. Teasels have not yet lost their purple sweatbands, nor thistles and burdocks their purple crowns.

Chicory

GR photo

Where the woods reach the road margin wild grape festoons the trees and fence rows and jewelweed, with its yellow and orange blossoms, rises in the shade. These flowers will soon dry into touch-me-nots that will explode seeds when you break this rule. My appreciation for jewelweed is tempered by having hiked through fields of them drenched to the shoulders from their retained dew.

On this hot sunny day wild animals are less in evidence. My count is only in identifiable road kills. Commonest — or unluckiest — are raccoons, perhaps one every 30 miles, but I also find two opossums, a woodchuck, a fox, a painted turtle, and a cat. Not a single skunk.

Although I drive with windows open, I hear few birds nor are many to be seen. But at one brief stop I identify the distinctive chirp of my first Henslow's sparrow of the year.

I will come this way again.

21. MOCKINGBIRD

September 2, 1991

Northern Mockingbird

My wife's father, James Theodore Copeland, a lifelong teetotaler, knows the mockingbird's song by a bit of doggerel, designed, I am sure, to shock his wife and daughter:

> *Theo, Theo, Theo:*
> *Get dressed, get dressed, get dressed;*
> *Go to town, go to town, go to town;*
> *Get drunk, get drunk, get drunk;*
> *Puke, puke, puke.*

In his rich southern accents that line is drawled into pea-uke, pea-uke, pea-uke. And the verse ends:

> *Shame, shame, shame.*

I can think of no more charming way to remember the mockingbird's thrice repeated phrasing, but no rhyme can convey the full repertoire of this versatile songster.

As I write this I sit on the open porch of my in-laws' home in north Alabama listening to a mockingbird sing into silent awe several brown thrashers who share its territory.

Mockingbirds mimic a wide range of the songs of other birds. Some of their copies are so close that electronic analysis cannot distinguish them from the original. One was recorded at the Cornell Laboratory of Ornithology imitating 30 species. Here in western New York Willy D'Anna, Patrick O'Donnell, and Betsy Potter found one mimicking 27 species just last year. But the all-time record seems to have been established in 1924 when C. W. Townsend reported a mockingbird that mimicked 55 species in one hour!

This one sticks to its local neighbors. It occasionally mixes in variations on the notes of oriole, pewee, red-eyed vireo, and towhee, but three it has down pat and imitates often. They are the Carolina wren's teakettle, teakettle, teakettle; the crested flycatcher's whirr, whirr, whirr; and the tufted titmouse's peter, peter, peter.

A light rain falls. Bob-whites, meadowlarks, and a cardinal call in the distance. A loggerhead shrike, a threatened species in New York State, hawks the field from a dead tree across the country lane. Four attractive birds of varying shades of blue are to be seen within a few yards of the house: blue jay, eastern bluebird, indigo bunting, and blue grosbeak.

But the mockingbird remains at center stage.

For a time he sat on the highest snag of a woodpile in a neighbor's yard, but now he sings while perched motionless on a phone wire a few yards from the bluebird. He could command attention with the flashes of white in his wings and tail as it flies or displays, but he doesn't need that now. His voice carries full effect.

Nesting territories have long been established so this bird can hardly be announcing his domain. Rather, I believe, he is simply singing for enjoyment. He has been at it all day and he even sang at intervals before dawn this morning.

Another mockingbird feeds now perhaps 50 feet away in a recently mown field. I have seen only the reddish egret use a similar technique. The mockingbird fans out its wings showing their contrasting dark and white areas, watching intently as it does so. The motion and the shadow it produces evidently frightens insects into moving, because the bird follows these displays by refolding its wings, hopping forward, and picking insects from the tufts of grass.

Starlings feed nearby. They drill deeply into the sandy soil possibly for Japanese beetle larvae. Even though they share the restaurant, the two species evidently read from a different page of the menu.

Listed as a rare visitor by Beardslee and Mitchell here in western New York in 1965, the mockingbird is still uncommon on the Niagara Frontier. Its numbers have, however, increased through the recent spell of mild winters, especially along the Ontario plain west of the Niagara River. One or more mockingbirds have been found regularly for several years in the hedges above the public boat landing in Lewiston. Like the cardinal before it and now with the Carolina wren and the tufted titmouse, their northward spread is assisted by those who feed birds through the winter.

Plant berry bushes or add apple slices to your feeder and you might attract one of these delightful birds.

22. ANT MAN

September 9, 1991

E. O. Wilson
Public Library of Science photo

Edward O. Wilson, Harvard entomologist and two-time Pulitzer Prize winner, spoke at the Buffalo Museum of Science shortly after this column was printed. His talk was on problems related to biological diversity and on ants, arguably the most remarkable of all insects.

No one who has been fascinated, as I have, by Carl Stephenson's short story, "Leiningen versus the Ants" or the non-fiction narratives about army ants like those of William Beebe, Arthur Loveridge, and Albert Schweitzer, could fail to be drawn to this subject. Here are these tiny insects (for even the larger army ants are only about a half inch long) driven entirely by instinct, yet able to do battle against intelligent man — and often win!

Those of you who have fought carpenter ants in your homes know something of this subject. Increase the size of those invaders, multiply their numbers to the millions, add to the soldiers sickle-shaped or toothed biting pincers whose spread is almost half the ant's length, witness their approach in a front about 40 feet wide destroying every living thing in their wake, and you have the army ants of tropical Africa and America.

Mark Twain spoke of these ants, "which vote, keep drilled armies, hold slaves, and dispute about religion." Not quite. But their activities are so remarkable that many early observers incorrectly assigned them a high level of intelligence. They overwhelm and kill animals thousands of times their individual size: even elephants flee them. By weaving their bodies together they construct elaborate bridges across streams or down the face of cliffs. They transport their entire colony – queen, eggs, young, food – along their line of march, alternately bivouacking and moving on. And, although blind, they communicate complex messages through smell: recognition, direction to a food site, alarm, and many others.

Careful research has demonstrated, however, that all of these activities are carried out by individual ants that are extremely limited in their abilities to act and react. For example, Wilson found that a dead ant gives off a specific odor. Noting this scent, other ants carry their dead comrade off to a refuse pile. He painted a live ant with this same smell. Nest mates grabbed it and carried it, kicking furiously, off to the refuse pile. The ant was allowed to return only after cleaning off all traces of the death odor.

Thus we can think of individual ants as programmed to respond to stimuli in very specific and predictable ways.

Maxis, a company that invents and distributes computer simulation games, is currently developing "SimAnt" based on this programmability. The game allows players to manipulate ant colonies by controlling these stimuli. They have loaned me an advance copy of this program that I find intriguing – although, as with most such games, I lose: my colony is invariably wiped out. This kind of "game" clearly has educational and motivational values for youngsters that go far beyond the usual zap-the-monster types.

*

Wilson derived from his research on ants and the work of colleagues on apes theories about genetic bases for some human behavior. Among the patterns he suggests are inherited: fear of the dark and of heights; immediately recognizable facial patterns that show such emotions as love, concern, anger, and hate; dietary preferences; taboos against incest; the peculiarly human kind of altruism displayed in acts of self-sacrifice; and the tendency to assign others to the categories of either friend or foe.

Although the storm has largely abated, the very thought of human conduct related to heredity was initially greeted with howls of protest. Critics claimed that Wilson's ideas, now given the name sociobiology, would justify inequity and exploitation. But Wilson himself had warned of exactly such misinterpretation. Instead today his work adds significant insights into the balancing effects of environment and genes on human activity.

23. MOLE

September 16, 1991

A Star-nosed Mole
Kenneth C. Catania photo*

Recently my friend, Jim Collins, told me about his garden problem. I am certain that his story will resonate with many of you as it did with me.

It seems that Jim's lawn was attacked by a mole this summer.

Now Jim knows that the generally beneficial mole was after the larvae of other invaders like Japanese beetles, but that didn't make his lawn any less unsightly. Long ridges trailed in uneven paths across open areas. They raised the ground high enough that his lawn mower dug dirt as it passed over them.

Like any other suburban homeowner, Jim's first response was to rush off to the nearest nursery where he would ask the experts what to do.

"Moles?" the clerk responded, "We have just the thing. These will drive moles or shrews from any yard." And the young woman led Jim to a shelf on which lay dozens of what she called "sure-fire mole removers": in less imperative terms, smoke bombs. Jim bought one of these overpriced firecrackers.

As you might expect, the result was not as advertised. The tube, carefully inserted into the tunnel and ignited, did produce smoke. Billows of it escaped, clouding the yard and for a short time leaving Jim as well as on-looking family and neighbors coughing in the acrid blue haze.

The next morning a dozen additional feet of tunnel announced the effect. Jim envisioned the mole smiling to itself as it tunneled on.

Angry now, Jim decided to give the experts one more chance. He returned to the nursery.

Another clerk this time: "No, those don't always work, but we have something here that will." And Jim was shown a vicious looking steel trap that would drive nail-like prongs into "any mole that continues to tunnel," the young man assured him.

In thinking back on the sequence afterwards, Jim realizes that he was manipulated. The smoke bomb serves to get the customer embarrassed and angry. Only then could he be convinced to use such a medieval torture device.

But feeling pressed to do something, he bought one of these fiendish instruments, took it home, and, carefully following instructions, set it over one of the trails.

It was, he admits, with some relief that he found, day after day, no results. Not entirely unhappily, he added this iron maiden to the other useless devices on the upper shelf of his tool shed.

The trails continued to extend. His yard looked like a U.S. map with highways crisscrossing the nation. And the neighbors no longer laughed out loud: they simply smiled.

Resigned to his fate, Jim told his story in a phone conversation with his father in Massachusetts. His dad suggested what Jim was certain was a ridiculous answer to his problem, but he decided in his extreme circumstances to try it.

He bought a large tin of V-8 juice, served the contents to his family (not part of his father's plan), and carefully buried the empty can in one of the mole's tunnels, its open top at the level of the tunnel floor. His dad had told him that the nearly blind mole would simply drop into the pitfall and be unable to climb up its slippery sides.

Sure enough, the next morning there was the mole at the bottom of the tin busily scratching at its cylindrical prison wall.

Although Jim told me that he was sorely tempted to deliver the little burrower to the yard of one of his more condescending neighbors, he freed the mole in a distant woodlot.

Cost of expert lessons: $21.58. Cost of solution (including the healthful drink): $1.15.

Now Jim says, he's tamping down the ridges in his lawn, waiting for the bare spots to appear where the remaining beetle grubs do their root damage, and hoping that starlings will solve this problem free of charge.

———

* *Professor Catania is a Vanderbilt University psychologist who studies the sensory systems of mammals, including the star-nosed mole. In a paper about this remarkable beast he writes, "The star-nosed mole (Condylura cristata) has a snout surrounded by 22 fleshy and mobile appendages. This unusual structure is not an olfactory organ, as might be assumed from its location, nor is it used to manipulate objects as might be guessed from its appearance. Rather, the star is devoted to the sense of touch, and for this purpose the appendages are covered with thousands of small mechanoreceptive Eimer's organs. Recent behavioral studies find that the star acts much like a tactile eye, having a small behavioral focus, or "fovea" at the center — used for detailed explorations of objects of interest."*

24. BIG NOSES

September 23, 1991

Black Skimmer

In early September we are spending two days on Long Island counting big noses — more accurately gull sized birds with big beaks — that are rare on the Niagara Frontier.

Our hosts, Tom and Diana Killip, take us on a tour of the barrier beaches from Jamaica Bay to Montauk Point, but most of our time is spent near the Atlantic Ocean outlet of Shinnecock Bay.

Our first big nose, the American oystercatcher, is an awkward appearing shorebird with a heavy plover-like shape. It has an overall black and white appearance, the black head color extending to the throat as well leaving only the belly white. It stands on heavy gray legs. More prominently it also has a thick orange bill fully twice as long as the rest of its head.

To me the appearance of this bird places it somewhere between silly and ugly. But what does it care. To another oystercatcher I am certain that it is a handsome specimen. And the massive bill is important. As the tide retreats, clams are exposed in the sand. When one of these bivalves relaxes its shell to take its first (and last) breath of air, the oystercatcher steps up and, its bill serving its role perfectly, neatly slices the tendon that holds the two shells so firmly together. A few quick scoops and the oystercatcher has eaten the exposed delicacy. No shore restaurant serves fresher blue points.

The second of our big noses is the black skimmer. A dozen of these slim tern-like birds with black backs, white throat and belly, and short red legs stand close together on an exposed sand bar facing into the wind. So far not very unusual, but now add to each bird a heavy, bright red, black-tipped bill even thicker than the oystercatcher's and as long as the bird's head and neck together. The lower mandible is bigger and a full inch longer than the upper. This bird has (switching metaphors) the strongest underbite since King Kong. It stands with body horizontal, appearing weighted down with this outsized beak.

But now one skimmer takes off on wings spanning four feet. It quarters over the only inches deep tidal waters. Sailing rapidly and under the perfect control of these powerful wings, it tips forward and plows the end of its lower bill along the unruffled, soft blue surface of the bay, leaving a tiny motorboat-like wake. Every 15 to 20 yards it scoops up a minnow and with a well practiced head motion neatly aligns it to be swallowed. The water is so smooth that, when the bird's bill is raised from the water to do this, we see an inverted bird reflected below. Now when it reinserts its bill into the water the skimmer and its reflection appear to kiss.

All of the awkward appearance of the standing birds is gone and we have a beautiful black, white, and red bird in perfect harmony with its environment. Standing it was Jimmy Durante, in flight it is Kevin Costner.

Our third big nose is more a Pinocchio than the others, for the even longer bill of the marbled godwit is at least slim. If we extend the Pinocchio analogy, the godwit must be one of the most spectacular liars of the bird world.

It is another shorebird, appearing still chubbier than the oystercatcher. Unlike the others, this bird is brown, in appearance like a larger, longer-billed yellowlegs. The bill is slightly upturned and 2 1/2 times its head length. One of the two we see conveniently raises its wings to show distinguishing cinnamon linings.

In the evening away from the shore we even find a fourth big nose, the smaller American woodcock. I leave this timberdoodle to a well-deserved column of its own.

25. DAVID BIGELOW

September 30, 1991

My predecessor, David Bigelow, a serious biologist

Photo courtesy of *The Buffalo News*

I never met my predecessor in writing these columns, Dave Bigelow. In fact I never even had the opportunity to read one of his columns until after his death. But I have now come to know Mr. Bigelow quite well through conversations with a few of his many friends and through reading about a quarter of his over 450 columns in the libraries of *The Buffalo News* and the Beaver Meadow Nature Center. I am clearly honored to follow him and his predecessors, Bob Wagner and Dick Burke.

It would be easy to write much about Mr. Bigelow: archaeologist, botanist, conservationist, educator, entomologist, falconer, museum curator, scout leader, writer, and zoologist, who incidentally fought as a sergeant with the VIII Corps from Normandy across Europe in World War II. But others have already done that very well. Instead I recall this lovely man through his own words. Here are four brief seasonal passages from his columns:

Spring: "Just then something else caught my eye beyond the glass patio door. For a moment I thought it might have been a maple leaf floating erratically in the wind, but there was no wind. When I stepped outside to feel the warmth of that glorious day, the 'leaf' appeared once more, settling upon the damp earth.

"As I had already begun to suspect, this drifting leaf turned out to be a butterfly, a beautiful Compton tortoise shell, which like its close relative, the mourning cloak, spends the winter not as a chrysalis but in hibernation."

Summer: "Poets have described 'the torching of red-berried elder' in early summer. Right now, the orioles, robins, and catbirds can be seen gorging themselves on those crimson fruit, while black-berried elder have suddenly burst into bloom. It is only among the flower clusters of black-berried elder that we occasionally find a truly spectacular long horn beetle. This gorgeous insect sports iridescent blue wing covers with golden yellow shoulder patches."

Fall: "Somebody called my attention to a very beautiful wood frog resting among the fallen leaves. Its beige skin tones so perfectly blended with those surroundings that I failed to see it until Mary Ann Snyder gave that frog a gentle nudge. Then I recognized Janice's favorite amphibian, a plump wood frog with dark masks over its eyes – like those of a raccoon. Almost numb from the chilling rain, this handsome frog soon will head for the muddy bottom of my neighbor's pond to hibernate with others of its kind."

Winter: "The next winter two raccoons discovered the entrance hole the squirrel had made in the wall above the basement stairs. Here the raccoons decided to spend the winter. Most often our sleep was interrupted around 2;00 a.m., when those noisy raccoons would commence a hockey game with one of those walnuts in our ceiling. Like most hockey games, these ended in a nightly brawl."

*

It is appropriate to add just one of his comments about teaching: "The success of a nature walk does not depend on how far we travel

74

or how fast one goes. What really counts is how much we can see in a relatively short distance. In leading my Saturday groups at Timber Trails, the object has always been to show people how to observe the things which are happening in the constantly changing world of nature, and to recognize the significance of each living animal or plant which we discover on these interpretive nature walks."

*

Perhaps his own most fitting epitaph Mr. Bigelow wrote when he lost a member of his family: "I beg the readers' forgiveness for the solemn thoughts of today's column, and promise to move forward into light and enjoyable adventures which the summer should hold for all of us. I'm most anxious to share some amusing anecdotes, but not today. You will understand."

I too understand.

26. ESCAPE

October 7, 1991

Orange-fronted Parakeet

Bill Eaton's home and next door antique shop are on lower Elmwood Avenue, but his backyard is a tiny park in the heart of Buffalo. Surrounding his small in-ground swimming pool are a number of 20 to 30 foot evergreens.

When I arrived last week in answer to his phoned invitation, Bill took me to a kitchen window opening on this yard. He then went outside and spread several scoops of wild bird seed on the tile surface beside the pool.

Before he even reentered the kitchen, house sparrows flew down from his trees and, as the word spread, from farther away until almost 100 milled about pecking at the seeds.

I was surprised to find no house finches, our more recent immigrant, among the sparrows. Bill told me that he occasionally saw them, but it was clear that those blusterers had not been able to intimidate these house sparrows as they have at many suburban feeders.

But now joining the drab brown and black sparrows appeared a fashion plate, a slim, pastel blue bird. It was a parakeet – or more technically a budgerigar. And within a minute or two a second parakeet joined it, this one blue-green. Slighter and more wary than the sparrows, these miniature parrots still fed among them in close proximity.

Bill had called me to ask how he might capture these exotic birds. He feels – as I do – that they will not survive the harsher weather ahead. I referred him to Art Clark at the museum, who suggested that he bait a cage. Bill is in the process of borrowing a cage to do this. And he invites the owner who has lost these birds to reclaim them.

Although a parakeet appearing at a local feeder is unusual – and finding two is even more remarkable – such an event is not unique. Bill Burch told me about another 'budgie' that came to the Lenehan's feeder on Grand Island last year from May until at least December. That bird also associated with house sparrows.

Budgerigars, originally from Australia, have now established wild breeding populations in southern Florida and for that reason are counted (only when seen in that area) by bird listers. Among other parrots established in Florida, the much larger monk parakeet, has also made brief inroads into New York State. Unlike the budgerigars, however, this species poses a significant threat. In South America troops of monk parakeets do much agricultural damage, especially to fruit crops. To head off similar problems here, the bulky nests of the few escaped birds in this state are destroyed.

European Goldfinch

These observations remind me of a note I received last April from Carol Hildebrand of Newfane. At her feeder another foreign visitor, a European goldfinch, had appeared. This species is easily distinguishable from American goldfinches by the bright red patch on the front of the face, this red accented by surrounding crescents of white and black. The yellow in this bird's wing is also located in a different area from that of our goldfinch in winter plumage.

"He appeared to be very hungry and quite aggressive," said Mrs. Hildebrand. "He wouldn't share the feeder with the other finches."

Although I visited the Hildebrand yard, I was unable to find this bird. But in January 1990, I had seen one of these lovely finches at the Ronan's feeder in Arcade.

For a time several decades ago a small group of European goldfinches nested on Long Island. It is said that these birds were released by an illegal importer when authorities raided his New York City shop. The species still breeds regularly in the Bahamas. But the ones observed here, like the parakeets, are almost certainly escaped cage birds.

27. MAPLE LEAVES

October 14, 1991

**Photo taken from Mill Road in East Aurora, New York
by Marty Wanglein**

As I write this column, there is a report of brief sleet squalls. A fifth of an inch of snow has fallen, an early record for the Niagara Frontier. That minor incident will probably be hooted by the national media. It will feed the rest of the country's appetite for putting down Buffalo as the Point Barrow of the Lower 48.

Let them. And meanwhile, certainly against the wishes of our local Chamber of Commerce, let us keep to ourselves the delights of this region.

On two recent hikes in the townships of Machias and Farmersville, I found enough glorious scenery to set to rest all of this negative publicity that has accumulated over the years.

The Finger Lakes Trail that I follow cuts across the Southern Tier from west to east over sections of both state and private land, occasionally skirting farm fields or following country roads, more often passing through second growth forests of mixed pines and hardwoods. Glacier tilled gullies and ridges run perpendicular to the path, but here those slopes are neither steep nor long.

The hardwoods in this area are mostly maples but there are also ashes, beeches, basswoods, and even an occasional birch. The softwoods include pines, tamaracks, a few cedars, and in one woodlot along Stebbins Road several hundred 70 to 80 foot Norway spruce.

These spruce are so dense overhead that they shut out most of the light. At noon it seems like evening and the needle and cone strewn forest floor deadens the sound of my boots. The effect would be threatening if it weren't for the chickadees, nuthatches, and kinglets happily chattering, tooting, and buzzing among the high branches.

But these days the maples take center stage.

Where the trail passes through maple woodlots, the footpath is so thickly covered with fallen leaves that I can only follow the blazes that mark the route. It is like walking on a painter's palette. The leaf colors range from the primary reds and yellows of those newly fallen through ever deepening bronzes, browns, and even purple as older leaves lose their last traces of life.

In the center of the woodlots the maples are still green, but as I reach an opening in the forest the bright sun backlights a single tree whose colors cover half the spectrum from soft green through yellow and orange to deepest red.

I can only think of my friend Bob Bugenstein's tongue-in-cheek remark, "If you've seen one tree, you've seen them all." In an odd way this tree confirms that comment. It represents its botanic kingdom so well that you need see no other. I am reluctant to move on.

This is, of course, not the only beautiful tree that I find. Over the twenty miles I hike in two days, I observe hundreds. And each contestant in this beauty contest has its own unique attributes. One is mostly green but that green shades smoothly into a rich yellow section, some individual leaves displaying both colors. In another a barred owl hunches, its brown stripes and gray facial disk contrasting like a lapel pin with the orange and red around it. Still another is a patchwork quilt with, it seems, every color represented.

But the most spectacular sight I find as I reach the crest of Bush Hill Road and look down over the valley to the north. The sun is gone now and a light rain falls, but even that cannot dull the bonfire of color below. The reds and yellows flicker in the light breeze and even the distant smoke-like haze contributes to the metaphor of fire. The scene takes my breath away.

Remember, don't pass on this information! It would spoil our image.

28. BONAPARTE'S GULLS

October 21, 1991

Bonaparte's Gull

My behavior didn't strike me as especially odd, but you may disagree.

I am talking about my only ride on "The Maid of the Mist" through the rapids just below Niagara Falls. I was with my son and daughter-in-law who were visiting from Denver, each of us suffocating in those lead-weighted yellow slickers.

As the boat chugged toward the base of Horseshoe Falls, the attention of everyone on board was riveted on the cascade of water falling closer and closer. Everyone except me, that is. I was turned away watching a few gulls that were as inattentive to the nearby falls as I was.

They were not the gulls that we see more and more often away from Lakes Erie and Ontario. Especially when storms threaten or fields are plowed, ring-billed and herring gulls congregate inland. And they have discovered fast food too. Near any restaurant dumpster you are almost certain to find a few. Already some youngsters think that MacDonald's trademark is two arches with a gull standing on one of them.

These gulls below the falls were smaller, less than half as bulky as even ring-billed gulls. When they rested on the water, they were also more buoyant than the bigger birds, sitting head erect, bodies riding high in the water. Their erratic flight pattern made them seem still lighter. Darting first one way then another, only occasionally dipping to the water to pick up a minnow, they seemed to have no care in the world.

They were Bonaparte's gulls, a special favorite of mine. This species is commonly seen along the Niagara River during spring and fall migrations.

*

I was reminded of this experience when I went to Squaw Island in the Niagara River last week to try to locate a rare Sabine's gull that had been reported there. I found no Sabine's but did see dozens of these Bonaparte's gulls patrolling up and down the river together with some equally graceful common terns. The number of these gulls will increase through the fall until harsher winter weather will drive them west through Lake Erie.

Because of their similarities and many plumages, gulls present identification problems. Like most others, the Bonaparte's body color is white, its back light gray, and its wing tips black. In breeding plumage adults have striking black heads, but even this is not diagnostic. Other less common gulls like the Franklin's, little, black-headed, Sabine's, and laughing gulls share this black hood. But at this time of year few of these birds retain the hood anyway. Instead their heads are all mostly white, the Bonaparte's, little, and black-headed gulls with a black dot behind the eye.

Especially in flight, the adult and immature "Boneys," as birders call them, appear quite different. Many first-time observers think that they are seeing two distinct species. The adult appears very light with a distinguishing white leading edge to its gray-mantled wings. The immature birds are just as handsome. Their wings are outlined in black and the tips of their tails are black as well.

*

French Emperor Napoleon I had a nephew named Charles Lucien Bonaparte. Unlike other members of this family whose energies turned to government and warfare, Charles chose a career in science. When he was in his early twenties, he moved to a home near Philadelphia, where, beginning in 1825, he published four volumes supplementing Alexander Wilson's *American Ornithology*. Despite his brief five years here, Charles Lucien Bonaparte has been called "the father of systematic ornithology in this country." His name is memorialized in that of this lovely little gull.

Here locally birders look for Bonaparte's gulls from the boatyards, the fishing piers, and the scenic overlooks along the Niagara River. It is, however, during migration a rather common bird of inland waters across the United States. This species should at least partially restore your appreciation for this opportunistic bird family.

29. CHARLES DARWIN

October 28, 1991

**1853 Pastel of Charles Darwin by Samuel Lawrence
drawn before the 1859 publication of *Origin of Species***

Western New Yorkers will recall the time when this was written as a brief period of football supremacy for the Buffalo Bills. They were division champions for four years and missed one Super Bowl win by an infamous "wide left" field goal kick. One of their fine players at that time was tight end Pete Metzelaars who plays a role in this column.

Dear Pete Metzelaars,

A reader has forwarded a report about your dancing over Charles Darwin's tomb in Westminister Abbey when the Bills played in London, because you thought he had "stupid theories."

I have high regard for your team and I regularly cheer your own contributions to their success. Also it has been years since I even coached football, so I hesitate to confront a young man a third my age and twice my size. Yet your comment provides an opportunity to speak in defense of one of my heroes. I seek to change your mind about Darwin who, I believe, stands with Galileo, Newton, Copernicus, and Einstein as one of the most important scientists of all history.

HMS Beagle
1851 watercolor by Owen Stanley

In *The Voyage of the Beagle* Darwin recorded a great adventure story: the narrative of his five-year trip around the world as naturalist aboard a small British navy surveying vessel. I urge you to read this book about the experiences of a young man your own age – for when he set out in 1831 Darwin was 22. For example, he spent months ashore in South America dodging bandits and experiencing a major earthquake. But it was also on this trip that his systematic observations of fossil and living animals, especially the tortoises and finches of the Galapagos Islands, shook his belief in the accepted biology of his time.

Darwin was a typical Victorian with strong religious convictions. He was also cautious and retiring, often ill. But the research he did upon his return to England on such diverse subjects as corals, pigeons and barnacles further convinced him of the evolutionary basis of species development. In 1859 he published his theories in a book that shook the world: *On the Origin of Species*.

In superficial summary, Darwin said that species evolve in response to competition and from the sum of their adaptations to their environment. Although we usually think of his theories applying in the wild, the breeding of flowers, dogs and agricultural crops offers even clearer evidence for this process.

It is important for you to know, Pete, that today almost all practicing scientists accept Darwin's general ideas, although some differ about the mechanisms that support evolution. Still more important, you should understand that there is not a forced choice between evolution and religion. In fact, two Catholic priests were among the witnesses Clarence Darrow sought to have testify in the 1925 Tennessee "Monkey Trial" of the high school biology teacher, John Scopes. (Scopes "crime" was telling his classes about evolution.) Indeed most churchmen as well as scientists today see faith and science as two different noncompeting realms or magisteria as Stephen Jay Gould has termed them.

But at the time of publication of his book it created a storm of controversy. Darwin stayed out of the limelight, quietly continuing his own research and writing; however, others defended him. In a famous debate Bishop Wilberforce – known as "Soapy Sam" in his time, he would today probably be a televangilist – scoffed at anyone who "believes himself to be descended from a monkey." Thomas Huxley famously responded that he would prefer to be descended from a monkey than from a bishop "who can put his brains to no better use than to ridicule science and misrepresent its cultivators."

As a recipient, Pete, you certainly know more about hero worship than I do. But I hope that there is room in both of our hearts for esteem for patient workers like Charles Darwin who change the course of humanity. Theirs may be a different kind of adulation from what we offer sports figures, movie and television stars, and rock musicians, but it will surely be less transitory. I hope too that we can find a lesson in Darwin's modesty in the face of both adulation and vilification, responses you yourself confront when you win and when you lose.

Meanwhile, I honor you for your great play. Go Bills!

30. BLOW-DOWN

November 4, 1991

Try carrying a canoe through this

With a hurricane whirling off into the North Atlantic as I write, I am reminded that I am all too familiar with the effects of strong winds on forests. Back in the 1950s I was on a canoe trip when the tail end of a hurricane swept through Algonquin Park. The most difficult trail I ever portaged was the half-mile carry from Happyisle Lake to Lake Opeongo on that trip. Normally this trail was an easy open path, but there were so many down trees that it was like carrying a canoe through a randomly twisted jungle gym. Even when I wasn't climbing over or under tree trunks, I had to fight strong wind gusts to keep my boat in line with the trail.

The wind was still blowing furiously when, as I struggled by yet another obstacle, I heard the crack of a tree trunk breaking. When you carry a canoe upside down on your head and shoulders, you see very little around you, so the sound of the falling tree became increasingly frightening. It had to be a giant: I could hear it breaking off other big trees as it fell toward me through the understory.

As the sound came closer and closer, I dove forward onto the path, the heavy canvas canoe banging down hard, thank goodness only partly against my back. An instant later the big tree hit too. Fortunately it had fallen parallel to the trail, its heavy thump so close that the ground shudder seemed to bounce me up an inch or two. It took several minutes for my panic to subside enough to let me raise my canoe and go on.

So I know about blow-down and I expect to find down trees when hiking in the spring before those wonderful crews of foresters and volunteers clear the trails. But early this year I found evidence that was unlike anything I had experienced in the past.

I first noticed an east-slope hillside along the New York-Pennsylvania border with every third or fourth tree broken off at about two-thirds of its original height. It gave the slanting forest a strange appearance with all these light wood scars facing me.

What caused this? The prevailing winds in this area are from the west so that this was the protected side of the hill. But even an east wind would have broken the trees off away from me so that the scars would not have shown.

Then on another hike in the same area I found the trail strewn with the tops of trees. In pine and hemlock groves it was like walking through a lot where Christmas trees were being sold. It was the same with deciduous trees as well: the top ten to twenty feet of beeches, maples, and birches lying everywhere.

Usually the wind breaks off a tree near its base or even tips its whole root system over at ground level. It took me miles of hiking and mulling over this evidence to come up with an answer. As in those old mystery stories, at this point I invite you to consider the evidence to see if you can determine a reason for this phenomenon.

*

What misled me, I believe, was my tight focus on wind. I am convinced that the destructive force in this case was ice. We in

Buffalo missed the full brunt of the March ice storm that did so much damage to our south and east and especially in Rochester. There ice formed on trees that was from one to two inches thick! Especially on conifers this ice accumulation on upper branches simply became too much to bear and the tops snapped off. Meanwhile lower branches were partly protected from the ice until the tree crown broke away. By then the full force of the storm had abated.

This was, I suggest, just one more of those questions so often posed by the natural world around us. Some of those questions are complicated, nearly intractable, and have been solved only after years of study. But others are like this one, probably transparent to all but this tired hiker.

31. BIRD FEEDING

November 11, 1991

Purple Finch

Anyone can gain pleasure from feeding birds. When she was in a nursing home, my mother placed a few crumbs on an outside windowsill to attract sparrows and pigeons, their visits giving her hours of simple pleasure. My wife, also not a birder, speaks of "her" cardinal family, the "husband" escorting and sometimes feeding "his wife" beneath our feeder where chickadees and house finches have dropped seeds. (I have visions of a kingbird having conferred the blessings of ornithological matrimony on these two.)

Feeding can range from a few corncobs thrown on a patio deck or table to expensive triple plastic and metal towers containing specialized foods, some, like Niger seed, imported from foreign countries.

If you wish to begin feeding birds, my advice is to start simple. Don't buy expensive feeders that squirrels and raccoons will quickly destroy, in the process destroying your willingness to try again. Instead merely put out in an exposed place a seed mix that includes sunflower seeds. Or hang from a tree limb a small slab of butcher's suet in a string onion bag. Then be prepared for days or even weeks before birds discover your bounty, and for an initial concentration of house sparrows at the seed and starlings at the suet.

But if you prevail you will find more and more interesting birds visiting you. Often the first among these will be house finches, the sparrow-sized males with a rosy background to their brown streaks. Then sooner or later will come chickadees and jays and nuthatches and cardinals and juncos and mourning doves and less common birds until your interest is captured for all time.

My wife and I have several times graduated from simple feeders to the complex products of local garden stores, but each time we have been punished severely. Inevitably squirrels have gotten to those better feeders, knocking them down, chewing through the plastic, and making them useless. We now are back to a small satellite feeder mounted close under an inverted bowl, the strong nylon string that holds it tied to a high tree limb. It hangs about six feet off the ground, well away from the trunk of the supporting tree. Squirrels cannot jump to it from below and those that try to leap or slide to it from above are fended off by the bowl. Nearby a rubberized metal suet feeder is similarly mounted.

One of the problems with suet is that it turns rancid. Here is a recipe for a suet substitute, passed on to me by Mike Galas, that avoids this problem:

You will need ingredients in these proportions: 5 pounds of cornmeal, 1 2/3 pounds of flour, 1 pound of ground egg shells, 2 pounds of peanut hearts, 1 pound of raisins, and 4 pounds of lard.

Local feed stores carry the dry materials except for eggshells. To include them you'll have to collect and grind the eggshells yourself. It is possible to omit them, but grit is important to birds. They have no teeth and an abrasive in their craw is necessary for them to digest food. That is one of the things birds are after when you see them feeding along roadsides in winter.

Mix the dry ingredients in a large container. Melt and add the lard, blending evenly. Shape the mixture into suet balls, spoon it into forms that fit your feeders, or smear it on pinecones to be hung like ornaments from tree limbs. Refrigerate in baggies what you don't use immediately.

Locate your feeders where you can observe them from a kitchen, living room or study window. If you do this, you'll soon join the many thousands who derive great pleasure from their close and supportive encounters with their feathered neighbors.

32. KENN KAUFMAN

November 18, 1991

Boreal Owl

Kenn Kaufman, one of the outstanding field ornithologists of this country, spoke at the Buffalo Museum on November 20. His talk, "Owl in a Day's Work: How We Broke the World Owling Record," was the first William C. Vaughan Memorial Lecture, beginning an annual series in honor of this highly respected elder statesman of local birding who died in 1990. Cosponsored with the museum by the Buffalo Audubon Society and the Buffalo Ornithological Society, this series is open and free to the public.

Kaufman is author of one of the latest entries in the Peterson Field Guide Series. His *Field Guide to Advanced Birding* addresses serious identification problems, among them many of the most difficult look-alikes: greater and lesser scaup ducks; least, yellow-bellied, Acadian, alder, and willow flycatchers; purple and house finches. He also edited the "Photo Quiz" in the journal *Birding*, a column that gave him an opportunity to point out fine plumage distinctions — and incidentally to stump me every time.

As if to advertise Kaufman's talk, a rare boreal owl was spotted in Rock Point Provincial Park just a week before his visit. I joined dozens of Canadian and United States birders looking unsuccessfully for this little owl the next day after it was reported. We did find among the pines and spruces that decorate this park three long-eared owls, a gray phase screech owl, and a saw-whet owl. Several observers also found a snowy owl just west of the park at Lowbanks, but the boreal owl was not relocated. Non-birders would have found it strange to see people going from evergreen to evergreen, pushing aside branches and scanning the exposed trees from top to bottom. They might have guessed that these folks were searching for pine cones and they would not have been far wrong: the boreal owl, at 9 to10 inches, is the same size as the largest white pine cones.

But birders were not alone in searching the trees and brambles. A Cooper's hawk that had been patrolling the lakeshore suddenly dove into a thicket and carried off a robin-sized prey. This episode may have represented the demise of the owl we were seeking.

To the ancient Greeks Boreas was the god of the north wind and boreal is derived from this name. Biologists refer to the region of coniferous forests that circle the Northern Hemisphere as the boreal zone and this is exactly the home territory for the boreal owl. Across Canada this region extends from the northernmost east-west highways and railroads to the barren muskeg of the still farther north.

There are only about a dozen records of the boreal owl for New York State. Local birders who want a chance to see it and another rare species of the far north, the great gray owl, usually travel in the dead of winter to Amherst Island near Kingston, Ontario.

What then is this owl doing here now? That question is a difficult one to answer. One guess is that its appearance presages an eruption of northern species into this area this winter. The early appearance of several snowy owls, pine siskins, and evening grosbeaks here and some redpolls and bohemian waxwings near Toronto support this possibility.

Some believe that these periodic southward migrations of northern species are caused by poor food crops in their home territory: a bad year for pine cones, for example. More recently biologists have suggested that the opposite is the cause. A series of several years of good crops and mild weather lead to breeding success and inevitably overpopulation. Then even the good food supply is not enough and some birds are forced to emigrate.

Whatever the cause of these incursions, they provide extra excitement for birders, who will be on the lookout for these northern visitors in the winter months ahead.

33. OUR DEER PROBLEM

November 25, 1991

**Part of a Deer Herd in Allegany County, New York
near the Pennsylvania Border
GR photo**

I have followed with concern news reports about hunting and about deer over the past several weeks. These reports have included one about animal rights activists obstructing hunters, another about a hunter gored by a deer, still another about a "pet" deer illegally shot in a residential neighborhood, and finally one about destruction of rare plants by deer in the Reinstein Woods Sanctuary of Cheektowaga, New York.

It seems to me that all of these reports are related to the important problem of deer overpopulation in metropolitan areas. I seek in this column not to answer that problem but rather to bring to it a personal perspective.

The New York Department of Environmental Conservation's expanded hunting season will not reduce the deer population of the suburbs in most of which hunting is banned. Town councilors there face a no-win situation. Whatever they do will hurt them. On one hand they have residents complaining about destruction of their gardens and their highway departments concerned about accidents caused by deer wandering onto roads. On the other they have those who want no harm done to these attractive animals.

Worse will come. I predict that we will soon have a child severely injured. Few realize that a buck in rut is more dangerous than a wolf.

I have special empathy for those who must face this problem of overabundance, because I was in a similar position once myself as a member of the board of the Bergen Swamp Preservation Society.

Byron-Bergen Swamp is a wild tract of mostly hardwood forest along Black Creek about twelve miles northeast of Batavia, New York. Within this forest are two unusual biological types: hemlock knolls and marl bogs, the bogs providing a home for Massasauga rattlesnakes and rare wildflowers including many orchids. It was to preserve this rich biotic community that the society was established.

To do so the society had adopted a policy of full wildlife protection but now one protected species, the white-tailed deer, was destroying others: the very rare flowers the organization was established to preserve. We on the board agonized over this problem, deciding after lengthy deliberations to allow limited bow-hunting of deer within the sanctuary. This draconian measure saved several plant species from extinction, but it also cost the lives of a number of deer and the support of a full quarter of our membership.

Indeed the overpopulation is not the fault of the deer. It is our fault for inadvertently improving deer habitat as abandoned farmland reverts to woodlots and for destroying or driving out deer's natural predators. But as is so often the case, assigning blame for past deeds that could hardly have gone otherwise is of no benefit today.

*

On the day before deer season opened in New York, four of us paused to watch a five-point buck feeding quietly on vineyard grapes. I am certain that the same question occurred to each of us: Who would want to destroy this handsome and innocent beast?

It is exactly that question, however, that lies at the heart of this problem.

How much easier it would be if the deer were not so attractive. What if we replaced that lovely pelt with rough scales, the shoe button nose with a grinning crocodile's maw, the lovely brown of those pleading eyes with a baleful red, and the graceful legs with the threatening claws of a dragon? Of course we should be thankful that we cannot make those substitutions, but if we could perhaps more of us would be prepared to initiate the control measures that are so strongly demanded.

I do not mean to imply that sentimentality is a bad character trait. Who doesn't love Bambi? But now it is the message of that other deer story, *The Yearling*, that we should heed: Sentiment must give way to responsibility.

I wish well then to those who must respond to this difficult conservation problem. I urge understanding and forbearance from the rest of us.

34. CLOSING DOWN

December 2, 1991

One of the forms of club moss, *Lycopodium volubile*
GR photo

If the metaphor associated with spring is birth, that associated with fall should accordingly be death. And there is much death in the fall months. Many insects, for example, end their brief life spans at this time, the continuation of their species assured only by hidden eggs that will hatch next year. Annual plants die too, in their case with widely distributed seeds assuring new birth come spring.

Like most of us, however, I am not attracted to the image of death. I prefer to think of Nature as closing down for the winter in the same way that cottage-owners drain the water pipes, nail the shutters over the windows, and lock the doors for another season. Nature does not die, it only retreats temporarily.

This fall on my weekly hikes along the Finger Lakes Trail from Franklinville to Portageville I had the opportunity to watch this annual process.

Of course the major show was provided by the leaves of the hardwoods and especially the maples. This display was protracted this year with almost a month of splendor.

Then in late October when the maple display was over there was a brief reprise of bright yellow. This was the time for the tamaracks and aspens. Unlike other members of the pine family the tamarack or larch sheds all of its needles in winter, weeks after most of the hardwoods lose their leaves. But before they become brown and drop, the needles of these attractive trees turn briefly from their usual soft green to bright yellow.

And just at this time the leaves of the quaking aspen turn almost exactly the same brilliant yellow. Quaking is a perfect name for these trees, as these heart-shaped and finely saw-toothed leaves tremble in the slightest breeze. Because both the tamaracks and the aspens tend to grow in groups of their own kind, open hillsides with mostly brown bare trees at this season have streaks of yellow splashed across them. On one hill in Centerville these yellow swaths alternated with the green of pines to further enhance their effect.

I watched too as the bronze and green of fields of goldenrod changed to dull brown, taking with them the lovely soft blues and violets of the late blooming asters and the still flowering chicory. If you look too closely at chicory plants, they appear gnarled and twisted, but from farther away they seem to me just as delicate and attractive as the asters.

Meanwhile the cattails softened and expanded, the milkweed pods burst open to disgorge their tiny hang gliders, and a few musk mallows and evening primroses bloomed limply well beyond their season into late October.

The fable of the grasshopper and the ant came to mind often as I listened to crickets chirping in November. Aesop's industrious ant, you will recall, busies itself readying for winter, while the grasshopper, living only for the present, is unprepared for the harsher season to come. And indeed these late fiddling grasshoppers and field crickets of this region have by now, as I write late in November, been struck down by the cold weather. None will live to see the eggs the females have deposited in the ground hatch next year. The ants on the other hand have retreated to their hill galleries in large numbers. Like bees their individual body heat will add to the temperature of the entire colony. They will remain dormant there until they emerge busy again next spring.

By mid-November the fall rains had turned the leaves of the forest floor to a slippery dark brown mass, the first stage of their return to earth as mulch. But some green remained along my path in the club mosses and the Christmas ferns. And in one low boggy area I even found a shaft of skunk cabbage forcing its green and white nose up through the duff. To me this provided the first pinpoint light of the spring that is at the end of the long tunnel of winter ahead.

35. CHRISTMAS COUNTS: 1

December 2, 1991

Snowy Owl

Through the 19th century anyone who studied birds seriously went afield with gun in hand. For example, the early bird artists, Audubon in particular, thought nothing of shooting dozens of birds of a single species in order make a field sketch for a painting.

Then in 1900, 26 bird watchers joined Frank Chapman, an assistant curator of mammals and birds at the American Museum of Natural History in New York City, on the first Christmas Bird Count. That field trip initiated what one ornithologist has called a "new epoch in bird study. It represented a first step in the replacement of the gun by binoculars and, more recently, the camera.

That single count in 1900 has also evolved into an annual international birding adventure. In 1990 there were over 1600 separate counts tabulated in 17 different countries with 35,000 participants taking the field. A total of 587 species were recorded in North America.

It was not until 1929 that a Christmas Count was mounted locally. In that year seven Buffalo Ornithological Society members in three parties counted 5300 birds of 31 species. For comparison, last year on the 61st repetition of this count 47 observers in 16 parties tabulated 64,000 birds of 73 species. The record number of species was recorded in 1969 when 86 were seen, and over the years a grand total of 146 species have been observed.

The rules for the Christmas Counts are strict. Each count is organized within a 15-mile diameter circle and within a date period from mid-December until early January set each year by the supervising National Audubon Society. Data is carefully recorded for each area, including not only species names and totals but also such details as party hours in the field walking and traveling by car. This latter information gives a measure of the extent of coverage provided. Clearly, for example, a single party afield for three or four hours could not census an area as completely as a dozen parties birding for longer periods. When all this data is compiled, it produces a hefty volume. The 1990 reports and commentary published in the journal *American Birds* filled 503 pages.

Today there are four local Christmas Counts. They are scheduled on different dates so that audacious birders can participate in several. Anyone interested in joining a count should contact the compiler soon at the phone number given to gain further information.

The Buffalo Ornithological Society's count center is on Grand Island and participants will census both the American and Canadian sides of the Niagara River from below the Rainbow Bridge to the Buffalo waterfront.

The Buffalo Audubon Society count is in its 46th. Its center is in Chestnut Ridge Park and the circle includes the area from the Southtowns to Boston and Coldon.

Third is a Canadian count whose center is in Queenston, Ontario. It overlaps well into the Lake Ontario plains in Niagara County. This Niagara count is in its 27th year. As with the Buffalo Ornithological Society count, Canadian and American observers participate.

The Beaver Meadow Christmas Count, now in its 18th year, centers on the sanctuary in Java and includes much upland country with open fields and scattered woodlots. Dave Junkin, director of the Beaver Meadow sanctuary, tells me that this census has been notorious over the years for difficult weather conditions, but that is a part of the winter study of nature.

If you join one of these counts, be sure to wear warm clothing and be prepared for intensive activity. But be prepared too for the satisfaction of contributing to our long-term information about the birds of this region.

You will see in column 38 that I omitted a number of western New York and southern Ontario, Canada counts from this listing, and since then a new count of Wilson, New York and the nearby Lake Ontario Plains has been initiated by Garner Light.

36. GRAY SQUIRREL

December 23, 1991

Eastern Gray Squirrel

She's a daily visitor. I watch her now in the early morning light, sitting upright under my bird feeder stuffing sunflower seeds into her mouth with her delicate forepaws. Her thick winter coat is salt-and-pepper gray shading into white on the chest and belly; white also rings her dark eyes. Tawny highlights are mostly hidden now but will begin to show again in spring when this rich pelt wears thin.

But of course her main feature is the beautiful fluffy gray tail that winds up behind her body and over her head. The genus of this gray squirrel is *Sciurus*, a perfect Latin name because it means "creature that sits in the shadow of its tail." She will use her tail for many things — signal, parachute, sunshade, umbrella, blanket — and soon she will demonstrate an even more important role.

That tail is nervously jerking now because she has seen me watching from the window. She disdainfully flicks it at me before she races up our ash tree, teeters along a phone wire, leaps into the larger oak, dashes down it head first, and bounds around a neighbor's house to another feeder where she knows there are better pickings anyway. All this way her tail flags from side to side. Especially apparent when she tight-roped that phone line, it is the balance pole of this high-wire circus artist.

Farther down the street and high up in a mature maple, she has a nest of leaves. They look disorganized, like a bushel-full that just happened to gather there, but inside that conglomeration the nest has a closely woven twig base with some moss and cedar fronds for a bed. The mass of leaves also looks too small to hold this twenty-inch squirrel, but its five- to ten-inch diameter interior chamber is not only big enough for her to curl up in, but will later hold her young as well.

A gray squirrel does not hibernate, but through winter's harshest weather she will sometimes remain in this nest with her tail wound around her for two or three days between feeding forays.

It is mating season now and she'll enjoy these few weeks of being wooed and chased by excited males. Most advances she'll rebuff, and just as well too, for soon after she is impregnated her consort will lose interest. She'll see him only at a distance until she's ready to mate again in a year or possibly even six months from now.

This female has fed well through the growing season and is in good condition. And she hasn't just eaten at feeders. She incurred the enduring antipathy of my wife last spring when she bit off and dropped foot long sprays from our red oak just to nibble a few of the tender twigs and buds. As the year advanced she dined on acorns, other nuts and berries, mushrooms, insects, and yes, when she could get at them, eggs and nestling birds. She didn't turn down carrion and, if she had been able to find them, she'd have enjoyed gnawing on deer antlers. If in the tougher times of the coming winter her other food sources are depleted, she will even turn to eating bark.

As if to offset that possibility, she continues to cache hundreds of nuts and seeds in tree hollows and more often in one to two inch holes she digs in our lawn and gardens. Her memory is excellent: we'll see her later this winter stop in mid-dash across our yard to burrow down through several inches of snow and earth to retrieve an acorn.

In early March she'll bear three or four pink, naked, half-ounce young that will grow rapidly in the nest until mid-April but won't be weaned for still another month. We'll watch those youngsters venture out to play along our juniper hedge next summer.

37. HUNTER'S STAND

January 6, 1992

A Black-capped Chickadee has taken a seed from my hand
Photo GR (taken with my right hand)

While hiking near Rushford, I came upon an example of modern technology supporting sport. It was a spanking new metal hunting stand mounted against a big beech tree. The beech tree was, of course, provided by the accommodating forest.

Like anyone who has spent time in the woods, I have seen hunting stands before. Usually they amount to a few boards or sticks nailed to a tree so that the hunter can climb to a low limb or fork. There he or she will stand or sit for hours, often cold and uncomfortably cramped, in wait for game. Sometimes the stands are more complex, perhaps a few more boards providing a kind of tree house, but never before had I seen anything as smart as this. Although this stand was made of aluminum, it still must have taken some effort to pack it in to this remote glade.

In appearance this stand looked like half of a children's slide – the stairs half. The steeply slanting gray steps were fastened to the tree with braces and straps midway up and at the top.

I climbed up these steps carefully — my purpose education, not vandalism. Reaching the top I clumsily turned and seated myself on the comfortable cushion. There was even a seat belt. This would be a must for someone like me: in this cozy position I would surely fall asleep almost immediately.

It was a delightful spot. I could see about 80 yards in three directions through the mixed open forest. This was an area where big old trees had shaded out the undergrowth. In addition to the predominant beeches and maples there were tuliptrees and basswoods and a few spruce whose lower limbs had died back leaving them standing like feather dusters among the table legs of the bigger hardwoods. The forest floor was leaf covered, providing a background of somber but not unattractive yellows and browns. Only the spruces offered a contrasting green.

As I sat for a few moments, a troop of small birds moved into the area and advanced from branch to branch nearby. They paid me little attention and it was a special pleasure to be with them up here in their world. First appeared a silent brown creeper hitching its way up a tree trunk. It was soon joined by noisier birds: chickadees whistling their high pitched notes and dee-deeing; a downy woodpecker wheeling to call "pick" at me as it flew past and then whinnying from a dead snag; and a nuthatch, whose nasal "yank" suggested a severe adenoid problem. A sentinel blue jay screamed from the higher branches. And finally I made out, well down the slope just where the trees began to blend together, a more reticent hermit thrush perched on a low branch.

Within minutes the fifteen to twenty birds were gone and the woods were again silent. Reluctantly I climbed down and hiked on.

I am not a hunter but I have many friends who are. This brief experience reminded me of my Rochester friend, Don Nelson, whose initial interest in birding came from his hours alone in tree stands. He had hunted for several years before he constructed and began using a makeshift stand in the Adirondacks. There he encountered birds from his lookout just as I had from this stand. Intrigued by them, he began carrying birdseed in his pocket and was soon able to feed small birds from his hand. Unable to identify the birds, he bought a field guide, carried it with him, and began to discover what species visited him in his forest hide.

He knew he was hooked on bird watching, he told me, when on one trip he discovered, after sitting on his tree limb for almost an hour, that he'd forgotten to carry his gun with him up to his perch. There it stood leaning up against the bole of the tree below him.

38. CHRISTMAS COUNTS: 2

January 13, 1992

Pine Siskin

Bob Sundell thought that he had chosen the best possible date for the Jamestown Christmas Count. It was December 15, the earliest Sunday in the count period defined by the National Audubon Society.

But when Bob rose at four that morning to join friends for pre-dawn owling, he looked out at a blizzard. A foot of snow blanketed his yard and another foot was to come before the morning was over. It took him almost two hours to shovel his car out of his driveway and he missed the owling entirely.

Owling is one of those strange things that bird watchers do in the dark. In the early morning or late evening a passing motorist will come upon several cars parked beside a woodlot. Several people stand by the cars, one or two of them whistling high pitched staccato notes or growling low hoots. When the motorist asks what they are doing, he is told, "We're calling owls." This response invariably draws a roll of the eyes and a headshake as the disbelieving driver speeds off.

Despite his miserable start, Bob described the 1991 Jamestown count as tied for best ever with 74 species, a half dozen more than in any recent year. That morning blizzard with its whiteouts broke up by noon to provide a pleasant afternoon of birding.

Among the unusual birds on the count were the first turkey vulture in the 55 year count history and the first bald eagle since the 1950s. Without him Bob's owling friends called up both screech and great horned owls.

The weather even helped. Among the more common birds at Carol Wagner's feeder in Lakewood were Carolina wren, pine siskin, golden-crowned kinglet and brown creeper, as well as a marauding sharp-shinned hawk.

As always, the results varied on the ten western New York Christmas Counts. None of the others faced blizzards, but compilers reported conditions that ranged from "miserable" to "not too bad."

There is, of course, the usual list of interesting birds. Buffalo's 78 species included eared grebe and common tern. Hamburg-East Aurora had 63 species, among them common loon and glaucous gull. The gull may have been one of the first attracted to a kill of gizzard shad, a kind of herring, in the South Buffalo harbor that later drew thousands of gulls to that area.

The loon was found on Green Pond in Orchard Park. Sadly it may not have been able to take off before this narrow stretch of water froze over completely. (Two rare white pelicans in Ontario's Jordan Harbor faced a similar fate as I wrote this column. They were, however, later rescued by some daredevil Canadian birders who crawled out on the ice to free them and then release them in open water.)

A Bohemian waxwing, a pine grosbeak, and 22 bluebirds were among the 62 species found in the United States part of the Niagara Falls count. In the Oak Orchard Swamp count there were 51 species with high totals recorded for many including 11 Cooper's hawks and 5 pileated woodpeckers.

Beaver Meadow's 51 species included a remarkable 9 barred owls. Among the 148 turkeys also found on this count was a possible albino. Hans Kunze, who recorded this bird, took a great deal of ribbing from his colleagues who believed that the white turkey was an escaped barnyard fowl.

Two goshawks were among the 49 species recorded in Scio and the St. Bonaventure count turned up a raven among its 43 species. Dunkirk-Fredonia had 54 species including snow goose and Letchworth-Silver Lake's 72 species also included a snow goose and 5 ruddy ducks as well.

Even the police participated, appearing at Bill Watson's Tonawanda home late on the Buffalo count day. Bill and I had focused our binoculars on a red-winged blackbird near an apartment building, which led one of the residents to report to 911 Bill's license number as "the car of two Peeping Toms." Fortunately the accommodating police were amused by his wife's explanation that we were "just bird watchers."

39. ARBORVITAE

January 20, 1992

A group of cedars in my backyard

GR photo

Imagine for a moment that you are a crew member with the French explorer, Jacques Cartier in the winter of 1535-36. You are very ill and you expect to die soon.

In the fall you sailed through the Gulf of St. Lawrence and up the St. Lawrence River to Hochelaga, a Huron camp. There Cartier climbed a height of land and named it Mont Real. But from that promontory he observed upstream "a sault of water, the most impetuous one could possibly see." That "sault" was the La Chine Rapids that effectively blocked your passage.

So your three ships retreated to another Huron camp, Stadacona, at the mouth of the St. Charles River where you have built a small fort. (In later years this will become Quebec City.) Earlier Donnaconna, the chief of these Hurons, had warned you that your trip to Hochelaga would lead to your death.

Winter arrived early and in full force. "From mid-November," Cartier will later write, your ships have been "frozen in ice thicker than two arms' length, and the snow piled to four or more feet."

And now early in the new year Donnaconna's prophesy seems to be coming true. You and every other crew member have become progressively sicker with "the pestilence." Already 25 of your original 110 have died and you are one of 40 more near death. Your legs are swollen and covered with purple blotches. Your gums are rotting and you can feel the few teeth you still retain loose in your mouth. You are in constant pain and can hardly see. Less than a dozen men are well enough to tend their dying shipmates: "a thing pitiful to see," records your captain.

Although the Hurons have been friendly, Cartier is afraid that they will take advantage of your troubles to attack. Under his orders and sick as you are, you must occasionally call out and clap rocks to suggest activity within the closed-off fort.

But now Donnaconna, who has recovered from the disease himself, tells Cartier of a tree, the anneda, that provides a curative. Indian women show the captain how to make tea by grinding the anneda's bark and fronds and boiling them in water. Cartier himself spoons out this evil-tasting potion, and you almost immediately feel miraculously better. "All the doctors of Europe," Cartier will write, "could not have done as much in a year as this tree did in one week."

The disease that beset you and your comrades was, of course, scurvy, the bane of anyone whose diet contains no fruit and vegetables that provide vitamin C. (It will be another 260 years before the British fleet is ordered to carry lime juice, effectively eradicating this dread sailors' affliction.)

The anneda, its evergreen foliage and bark both rich in this vitamin, will later be misnamed the white cedar for it is not related to the Old World and Biblical cedars.

Your captain is so impressed with its curative powers that he will carry specimens back to France. It will be the first native American tree transplanted to Europe. And based on this harrowing experience it will come to be known by a better name, the tree of life — arborvitae.

As I write, I can see through my study window a hedge of arborvitae across the street. They stand like green tenpins, conical and with a dusting of white snow. In swampy areas and damp forests they grow taller, in the open maintaining this compact cylindrical shape even when they reach 50 to 80 feet. Arborvitae are easy to identify by this shape, their twisted and shaggy trunk, and their delicate evergreen branchlets that are flat – they seem pressed – and yellowish.

I invite you to associate, as I do, this lovely evergreen, the arborvitae, with the salvation of those Hurons and 85 French explorers.

40. GROUNDHOG DAY

February 3, 1992

Our backyard woodchuck (aka groundhog) in a more congenial season
GR photo

Yesterday was Groundhog Day, the day the woodchuck (for the folklore is not specific to Pennsylvania's Punxsutawney Phil) is supposed to have awakened from its winter sleep and emerged from its den to stare bleary-eyed at the world around it. If it saw its shadow, it was frightened and staggered back to its nest to sleep through an additional six weeks of harsh weather. If it saw no shadow, an early spring is near at hand.

This story may be traced to European origins. In Germany the bear or badger awakens instead of the woodchuck, which only occurs in North America.

February 2 is also a religious feast, Candlemas Day, and there is an old English song that replaces legend with imperative:

> *If Candlemas be fair and bright,*
> *Come, Winter, have another flight;*
> *If Candlemas bring clouds and rain,*

Go, Winter, and come not again.

A meteorologist, if one were willing to respond to such lore, might suggest that a "fair and bright" (shadow producing) early February day could correlate with continuing cold and "clouds and rain" a thaw.

In any case Punxsutawney Phil is a very unusual woodchuck if he awoke this early. More likely he is just entering his last month of a five to six month period of hibernation.

If Phil was a wild woodchuck, he would have moved at the end of last September from a den along a meadow hedgerow to another he dug in a woodlot where the frost would penetrate to a lesser depth. He would then have retreated alone to his nest chamber filled with dry grasses two to four feet below the forest floor.

There he would remain, his 24-inch length curled down into a forward somersault, his forepaws folded across his breast, his nuzzle over them and against his stomach, his stubby seven inch tail to one side. With his eyes tightly shut, only his ears would show that this grizzled brown fur ball is an animal.

The hibernating woodchuck is not just asleep; his body changes have been profound. Like us, he would normally shiver and his metabolism rate would rise when his body cooled. His fur would fluff up to provide further insulation. But this animal has shut down the thermostat that provides these controls, allowing his body temperature to drop 59 degrees to only a half dozen above freezing. Instead of accelerating, his metabolism has slowed. The fat reserves built up last fall are depleted at a hundredth the normal rate. In five months he will lose only a pound or two, a little over a tenth of his weight but only half as much as he will lose in his first month outside before his favorite grasses and clover mature.

His tiny heart that normally beats 80 times a minute beats now only a half dozen times per minute. No detectable electrical signals emanate from his brain. And a remarkable six minutes pass between shallow breaths. One hibernating groundhog was not affected by spending four hours in a room filled with poison gas!

If you dug out his den and removed the woodchuck, you could bowl him about with no effect. Only a protracted warming would slowly wake him.

Yes, a woodchuck does occasionally leave its den in midwinter, but that animal will almost always die. It has usually come out because its fat reserves have been depleted. It may have been injured last fall and unable to store up enough fat, or a protracted cold period may have cooled its den too near to freezing, forcing its body to burn off this fuel. A vegetarian, it then has no access to its usual foods to make up this deficiency. It will starve if it is not taken by a predator.

Should you plan your next six weeks on the weather forecast of such an animal?

41. ROGER TORY PETERSON

February 10, 1992

In early 1992 an episode of the popular public television series, "Nature," was devoted to Roger Tory Peterson, the world renowned naturalist, artist and author who was born in 1908 in Jamestown and who spent his youth studying the insects, birds, flowers, and mammals of southwestern New York State.

It is difficult for all but the oldest of us interested in natural history to conceive of what it was like "Before Peterson," that is before the late 1930s when the first edition of his "A Field Guide to the Birds" became popular. Until then the best of the few available bird books, like the "Reed Bird Guide," had separate pictures of single species with accompanying text that gave little help in differentiating one bird from any other. For all but the most distinctive birds they were not useful for identification.

As a boy Peterson had read Ernest Thompson Seton's *Two Little Savages*, in which another youngster found mounted ducks in a museum and drew their silhouettes, distinguishing them through the use of arrows pointing to their unique features. Peterson remembered this and, when he wrote his bird guide, combined this technique with his own superb talents as an illustrator to produce what has come to be known as the Peterson identification method.

Today this method has been applied in over 40 Peterson *Field Guides* to everything from mammals to mushrooms, reptiles to rocks, and shells to stars. And every other field guide today has been influenced by Peterson's approach, even including military manuals for distinguishing aircraft and ships.

Now with little effort amateurs can identify most of the natural objects about them. As a result interest in natural history has burgeoned and the secondary effect of this increased interest on conservation has been widely recognized. Today's world would be measurably different were it not for Roger Tory Peterson.

Most naturalists think of Peterson only as an artist and fail to realize how good he was as writer and teacher. The text of his books is equal in quality to his illustrations. In less than a hundred words he describes a bird at rest and in flight, special features that separate it from similar species, different plumages, voice, range and habitat. If you think that is easy, try it yourself on a familiar species like a song sparrow.

When the 19 year old Peterson boarded the train from Jamestown to New York City to study art in 1927, few outside his family knew him by any other name but "Nuts." He was a shy loner. He had obtained permission directly from the police chief to stay out to collect moths past the strict town curfew for teenagers. He didn't date. With one or two friends he had wandered the countryside in search of wildlife. "Nuts" was a suitable name, the townspeople thought, for this other-worldly young man.

But 50 years later when he was approached by Lorimer Moe, Clarence Beal, Carl Hammerstrom, and a few others to assign his archives to Jamestown, "Nuts" Peterson remained loyal to this community. The Smithsonian Institution had held those archives temporarily and now placed a strong bid to retain them. Yale University offered a building already available on campus. Even against the cogent arguments of his wife Virginia, a Connecticut Yankee who supported the Yale offer, Peterson stood firm for Jamestown. And so the Roger Tory Peterson Institute is being built there.

Now we can continue to celebrate this native Western New Yorker, easily the best known naturalist in the world today, and the man who was even chosen by the citizens of his home town (but by just one vote over Lucille Ball) as "the most famous person to have ever come from Jamestown."

42. FRUIT TREES: CULTIVATED AND WILD

February 17. 1992

An aged Fruit Tree
GR photo

Presidents' Day gives me an opportunity to turn my thoughts to that casualty of young George Washington's hatchet, the cherry tree.

It will be almost three months before our orchards and woodlots will be decorated with those lovely cherry blossoms, as white as the snow that blankets everything today. That time will come but now may be a better occasion to offer some historical reflections.

The stock for all cultivated cherries in this country was originally imported from the Old World. There the history of cherry culture goes back to antiquity.

Wild sweet and sour cherries were from prehistoric times widely distributed through Europe and Asia and they were cultivated in China as early as 4000 years ago. Pliny, the first century historian, credits Lucullus for the first introduction of cherry culture to Europe in 65 BCE, the general bringing orchard trees back from a tour of duty in Asia Minor. But Theophrastus, who was called by Linnaeus "the Father of Botany," gave an account of their culture in Greece 250 years still earlier. In any case by the end of the first century cherries were a widely grown fruit crop across Europe and hundreds of varieties were propagated.

Probably the French brought those fruit trees first to eastern Canada at the beginning of the 17th century, but in 1629 Francis Higginson recorded Red Kentish cherries already being harvested in New England.

They made their way to New York State somewhat later. There are no records of their being grown here under Dutch rule; however, in 1665, after the English took over, Peter Stuyvesant, the Dutch director-general, retired to his farm in Manhattan's Bowery district. There he imported cherries and many other fruit trees and from that time their popularity was assured and they were widely grown. By 1915 Hedrick listed 1145 varieties of cherry in New York State. We know them in this region from the orchards along the Lake Plains of Erie and Ontario.

But wild cherries are native to the Western Hemisphere as well. The three found in this region are black cherry, chokecherry and fire or pin cherry. The latter two grow as shrubs or small trees but the mature black cherry can be 80 feet tall and ten feet around. Because this tree provides beautiful wood for furniture making, its numbers have been depleted and today very few mature stands remain. We are fortunate to have one of those groves in Cheektowaga's Reinstein Woods with some extending into Stiglmeier Park as well.

Black Cherry "potato chip" bark

GR photo

The dark trunks of all cherries are marked with many lighter brown or yellowish short horizontal streaks. The smaller branches of the black cherry have a distinct reddish cast and the bark of larger trees of this species breaks up into scales that Jeff Liddle, Reinstein Woods naturalist, aptly describes as burnt potato chips. If you look carefully, you'll still see the horizontal streaks on these scales. Deeper vertical cracks also expose the tree's reddish-brown underbark.

The blossoms of the black cherry and chokecherry are unlike those of the cultivated cherries. Their flowers appear in racemes, fronds similar to those of lilacs and quite dissimilar to the individual dogwood-like clusters of the cultivated varieties.

One of the distinctive features of both wild and cultivated cherries is the hydrocyanic acid contained in their leaves, twigs and seeds. A peeled twig has a musty or mildewed odor through which you can smell cyanide, the bitter almond scent will known to readers of detective fiction. Here then, in striking contrast to the tasty and wholesome meat of the cherries themselves, lurks a poison that under some conditions sickens or even kills livestock.

Although wild cherries were then common in Virginia, so too were imported strains and George Washington would probably not have been punished for cutting down a wild tree. Indeed he would have had great difficulty felling a black cherry with his small axe. His victim was almost certainly one of the trees in his father's orchard.

43. INSECT ANTIFREEZE

February 24, 1992

Mourning Cloak Butterfly

This species overwinters hibernating quietly underground

and is one of the first to emerge in spring

Karen Lee Lewis photo

When the temperature drops, you and I rely on mechanical heating systems to keep us warm, praying all the while that those systems will not malfunction and leave us at nature's mercy. We all know of homes where, in the absence of the owners, the heating system has broken down, pipes have burst and extraordinary damage has been done. Thus we also know that, should we lose heat when the temperature is well below freezing, we must stoke up the fireplace and prepare to drain our water pipes.

Animals are lucky. They don't have to worry about such complications. All they have to do is survive that cold first hand.

Marianne Moore and Richard Lee have written an interesting article in *American Entomologist* about how land and water insects respond to winter cold. Here are some of their observations.

Of course, a few insects simply avoid cold temperatures. Like some of us, monarch butterflies fly up to 1000 miles south. Other insects migrate downward. Some burrow into leaf litter or deeper into the earth below. Several water insects dig into pond sediments. Ground and ladybird beetles join large groups in rotting logs in order to share body warmth.

There is an interesting trade-off in burrowing into the ground. The deeper the insect digs, the warmer it finds its surroundings. But the insect doesn't have a calendar handy and needs the signal of spring's warming temperatures. It can't dig too deep for then it wouldn't awaken in time to utilize its full season in the sun. For this reason most burrowing insects are found in the top six inches of soil.

It may seem odd that snow serves as an insulator. A thick blanket of snow can raise the temperature at ground level dozens of degrees over that of the air above, but of course only up to the 32° temperature of snow itself. Thus a winter like this one with little snow cover is tougher on insects than one with deep snow.

Ice too provides insulation. The temperature of water below the ice of a stream, pond or lake is above freezing and increases with depth. Some aquatic insects like mayfly nymphs take advantage of this and retreat from shallow to deeper water as winter progresses.

But the biology of a few insects provides its own response to cold. Goldenrod gall worms withstand temperatures of -60°. In the high arctic some insects spend the winter on exposed rocks and the larvae of midges can survive encased in ice. The midges may find this necessary because, after prolonged cold, some shallow ponds freeze to the bottom.

For those of us who can never stay warm enough in winter, those facts are impressive. Even more impressive is how they are accomplished.

The secret of such insects' ability to withstand sub-zero temperatures is in their body's ability to "cold harden," a complex physiological and biochemical process by which their body synthesizes glycerol. In simpler terms they convert up to a quarter of their body fluids into antifreeze, providing them exactly the same cold defense that we give our car radiator.

But insects still cannot survive if their body fluids freeze. (This finding should send a message to those who believe what they read in science fiction about maintaining human life in frozen form.) And even those midges die in surface ice. Recall that ice expands as it freezes and hard ice crushes them. It is only in softer ice, called anchor ice, that they can sleep until spring melt revives them.

Interestingly, food in insects' stomachs can freeze and injure them too. It doesn't contain glycerol.

This winter with its warm and cold spells alternating is a difficult one for insects because it is forcing them to use more energy as their metabolism increases and decreases.

Let's hope it's killing off those mosquitoes now hiding in the leaf litter.

44. SIGNS

March 2, 1992

Eastern Coyote

Too long postponed, my first hike of the year along the Finger Lakes Trail starts at Whiskey Bridge, which crosses the Genesee River just south of Portageville, New York. I walk farther south along the river flats and then east up over the ridge toward Hunt.

There is a strong contrast between summer and winter hiking. In summer the woods along this trail would be lush and green, wildflowers of great variety would spread underfoot and the canopy would be full of songbirds. Today there is none of that. Where the ground is exposed, it is mostly a somber brown. Except for the few pines and hemlocks, the trees are dark leafless skeletons. No birds sing.

The only animal I see on this full day of hiking is a coyote. It eyes me from across a field, quickly identifies me as of no interest and turns to trot on about its business.

But winter hiking has its own values. There are fewer distractions, my attention not so quickly diverted. Smaller things take on importance and I have time to think about each observation, each incident. Indeed less does become more.

Winter is also a time for what trackers call reading sign. By this they mean reconstructing the past from what seem insignificant clues. Arguably the best tracker ever was Ernest Thompson Seton, whose vast experience in the wild allowed him to deduce, like Sherlock Holmes, complex stories from the tiniest of details. In one example, Seton showed where a rabbit fed on succulent twigs, but then dashed off, frightened, its strides lengthening until they stopped abruptly. There a deep indentation in the snow, a few drops of blood and wreath-like marks made by wings made clear to the author where an owl ended the rabbit's brief life.

I bring few skills to this kind of detection, but I enjoy the challenges that small observations provide. Most of the time I am left with more questions than answers, but I find speculation itself an interesting preoccupation.

Some evidence leads to obvious conclusions. What at first appear to be dark shadows that extend from the base of larger trees are really patches of bare ground. Their direction tells me that the recent snow squall came out of the west southwest.

There is just enough snow to make animal tracks apparent. Those of deer and rabbit are everywhere. It must have been a good winter for deer because they haven't even finished off all of the apples strewn about the forest floor near an abandoned farm.

Here are tracks of some member of the mustelid family, probably a weasel. I have occasionally seen weasels in winter when they are white with a black tipped tail, but not this year. Here a raccoon waddles along the side of a steep brook, its delicate, slightly turned-in forepaw prints clearly showing five fingers. And here is a skunk in a hurry, its footprint sets in diagonal lines.

But the more complex stories these animal signs tell are too subtle for me to decipher.

On my way back my curiosity leads me into a small cemetery where Bailey Road crests the ridge above the river. It is an attractive acre or two with hundred year old pines shading equally old gravestones. Here too I find sign. This time it is human sign.

A square pyramid marks the final resting place of a Gleason family: three sides identifying husband, wife and her mother. But it is the fourth stone face that attracts my attention. It reads:

EMMA

died Apr. 13, 1882

aged 19 years

JOHNNIE

died Apr. 13, 1882

aged 6 years

ETTIE

died Mar. 21, 1882

aged 3 years

Like those animal tracks this record doesn't tell me the whole story. It leaves me to fill in the details of this tragedy that took first the youngest child, the others lingering. I think of smallpox or a fire. And I think too of those stricken parents and grandmother who survived the children by dozens of years.

Death usually comes quickly and with finality in the wild. In our civilized world it more often haunts our memories as Emma, Johnnie and Ettie will mine.

45. BURDOCK

March 2, 1992

Earlier this afternoon when I returned from hiking and began to remove my outer clothing in the garage, I found my heavy wool socks and corduroy pants as usual strewn with unwanted souvenirs. They were again covered with burrs.

I spent the accustomed five minutes pulling off the tenacious seedpods.

Most often I find this an irritating task and grouse about the time wasted, but this once I thought about the special role of these carriers of life. It didn't make the job any easier but it gave me something to think about while I was doing it.

I find burrs remarkably opportunistic. Opportunistic? Surely not. That word implies volition, the burrs acting on their own initiative. And yet it is almost on the mark. They do seem at times to carry out purposeful actions. For example, when I pulled off several burrs that were embedded in my sock, one flipped up out of my hand to stick to the felt inside my parka hood next to my ear.

Even if such tricks aren't performed by design, the burrs are certainly engineering marvels. The inventor of Velcro must have been led to his discovery by an enlightened experience with these natural hitchhikers. It is amazing that anything so weightless can adhere so well.

Now at my desk I pull apart one of the spherical burrs. There is virtually no central body, the entire structure made up of half-inch needle-like bristles. Each bract is flattened at one end and has a tiny hook at the other, the hook so small that I have to use a hand lens to see it clearly.

When each needle is separated from the burr, the action releases a microscopic seed from its flat base. Even with that magnifying lens I can see these seeds only as tiny dots against the white paper on which I place them.

It seems at first as though there are thousands of these little crochet needles in each burr but a count of one shows that there are less than 200. Still for every burr that I have carried a few miles hiking and many further miles driving home, I am now freeing in a new location some 150 seeds and thus 150 potential new burdock plants.

Thus I am witnessing up close an extraordinary means of plant dispersal, another exhibit drawn from nature's overflowing bag of tricks.

In this region there are three species of burdock, the plant that bears these burrs. This morning I found an eight foot tall great burdock, twice the height of its cousin, the common burdock, this one broken at its base and lying in the snow like a leafless fallen tree. It was from this larger species that I unwittingly gathered the burrs I have described. Common burdock burrs are only a half-inch in diameter, those of this great burdock three times as large.

There is a less common third species, wooly burdock, intermediate in size between the others. It takes its name from a difference in its burr needles: they are covered with fine hairs.

All of these burdocks are biennials, that is their life span is two years. Through their first year they are low lying plants with large leathery leaves. I see those leaves regularly through the winter in roadside areas where the snow doesn't cover them. Only during their second year do the tall stems grow and produce rather attractive lavender flowers atop green clover-like balls. November cold erases those colors, the lavender florets falling away, the green balls turning to winter's brown burrs.

It is then that I and other wanderers across the fields aid in their seed dispersal.

Nature can play mean tricks in this process as well. I once found a dead morning dove lying in my path. Otherwise uninjured, it had a burr stuck between one wing and its body. This had effectively prevented it from flying and it had struggled its life away unable to free itself from those tiny but tenacious hooks.

46. BLUEBIRDS

March 16, 1992

Eastern Bluebird

I have a confession to make.

Many years ago I was a leader of an essentially one-man failed palace revolt. I sought to have the Eastern bluebird displaced by the kingbird as our New York State bird. It seemed to me that the regal kingbird was a more appropriate choice to represent the Empire State. And the bluebird was not unique to New York. We share it as state bird with Missouri and the closely related mountain bluebird represents Idaho and Nevada.

Of course my insurrection was immediately crushed and the lovely Eastern bluebird continues to represent us to this day. There are many arguments in its favor of this, but I recall only one telling criticism of my candidate. A discerning opponent felt that the kingbird represented one aspect of what he termed "our state personality" too well: our belligerence.

As punishment for that aberrant conduct, I have recalled that embarrassing episode every time since then that I have seen or heard a bluebird. Tarnished to this date is the exquisite pleasure of observing that soft blue back as a male flies off down a fence row, of hearing that distinctive mellow "chur-lee" call across the springtime fields.

This year I already saw three bluebirds in late February. On the 23rd two hunched together on a phone wire below the Niagara escarpment near Plank Road and a third graced an orchard tree just west of Dalton five days later. They might have been overwintering birds. Each year a few do stay through the winter months, changing their feeding habits from insects to fruit. But these birds all had the restless appearance of early migrants.

Of course my pleasure in those observations was again clouded by recall.

Thus in an attempt to propitiate for my brief affair with the kingbird, I devote the remainder of this column to Little Blue.

The timing is right. It has been proposed once again to modify Section 78 of the State Law, the legislation that names the state bird. But this time the legislation is in the bluebird's favor. It adds to the sentence designating the bluebird as our state representative, that it "shall be honored as such during the third week of March, which shall be known as 'bluebird week'."

This bill, co-sponsored by Senator John Sheffer as Bill 5580 (the corresponding Assembly Bill is 2180), now languishes in government operations committees in both houses. If you are among those who love this beautiful bird, you may wish to write or call legislators to indicate your support.

Added note: I have no idea what was the eventual outcome of that legislation. In seeking that information, however, I found that the Eastern bluebird had only been our New York State bird since 1970. Before that the designated species was the "robin red-breast."

A more direct way to contribute to the welfare of this species would be to build and set out bluebird boxes. A simple house plan calls for two 3/4 inch boards — one 4 by 30 inches and the other 5 1/2 by 27 1/2 — and about three dozen 1 3/4 inch galvanized siding or aluminum nails. Ten saw cuts, two holes drilled, some nails pounded and you have an assembled box. No painting necessary.

The house should be mounted four to five feet from the ground on a pole, fence post or tree trunk. It should be set out as soon as possible as bluebirds are already establishing territories.

Unfortunately for most city and suburb dwellers, bluebirds shy away from your area. They cannot compete there with starlings, house sparrows and house finches. Instead they are now truly country birds. They like open areas with a few trees and, since they often find insects on the ground, short-cropped vegetation. You find those conditions in pastures, golf courses, parks, cemeteries and near homes with large lawns. Those are sites where you should ask permission to place your nest boxes.

Finally, if you wish to join others who care for bluebirds, you can write for information to the Upstate New York Bluebird Society (Thomas Burke, 3013 Staley Road, Grand Island, NY 14072) or the North American Bluebird Society (Box 6295, Silver Spring, Md. 20916).

Please let this constitute a final payment for my attempted subversion and let me now simply enjoy these handsome and all too uncommon bluebirds.

47. MAPLE SYRUP

March 23, 1992

**Sugar Maple Forest in the Agawa Canyon
north of Sault Ste. Marie, Ontario
The hillside is very similar to that of Shadbush Farm**

Steve Eaton is a retired St. Bonaventure University biology professor who remains active on his Shadbush Farm east of Salamanca. There he tends a dozen beehives, raises blueberries, and manages a maple woodlot of 540 trees.

Early this month Steve let me spend a day with him as he processed 200 gallons of sap into just over three gallons of maple syrup. (He refined ten gallons of syrup the day before.)

I had offered to help out in exchange for the opportunity to learn about this activity, but my help consisted mainly of dodging out of his way as Steve calmly turned from task to task. He hauled firewood, stoked the fire, cleaned and filled the tanks, watched the level and characteristics of the roiling sap and syrup, constantly checked the temperature gauges, and at precisely the right time drew off pails of lovely brown liquid. Between other chores he found time to filter this syrup and decant it into quart jugs that look exactly like Appalachian moonshine crocks.

Carefully measuring the color of his syrup, he marked each cruet in this batch dark amber. The darker color signaled the approaching end of the season with only commercial grade syrup tainted by amino acids yet to come. Producers refer to this increasingly unpalatable later brew as buddy syrup, because it is associated with physiological changes in the tree as it begins to bud.

But now Steve offered me a spoonful of his still hot syrup. I found it delightful, the best I had ever tasted. After that I hovered close, fingering to my mouth the occasional spilled drop.

Maple trees are uniquely North American. Native Americans introduced them to the European newcomers, demonstrating how they poured sap into hollowed-out logs and added heated stones to boil away the water.

The colonists soon improved upon this process. Iron cauldrons replaced hollow logs. Later a series of heating pans were used with sap poured from one to the next as it thickened. More recently came enclosed evaporators like Steve's with channels through which the increasingly dense liquid flows. Today large producers use huge oil fired evaporators and add a stage of reverse osmosis to improve the processing still further.

One of these major producers, Randy Sprague, who taps over 14,000 trees in Portville, sold Steve this small 250-gallon evaporator, showed him how to use it, and continues to provide advice and assistance. Additional support, Steve tells me, comes from state and Western New York Maple Associations and from agricultural extension programs. He is clearly pleased with his friendly contacts through these groups with many dairy farmers who enjoy this "between seasons" activity.

As the fire slowly died from his day's operation, Steve led me up into his sugar bush to show me how he collected the maple sap.

When I first observed syrup making forty years ago they used buckets. It was only last fall, while hiking near Centerville, that I first met the kind of tubing that Steve used here. My path had been suddenly crisscrossed with a spider web of colored hoses and I first thought that I had come upon a new kind of fencing. Only when I found the big bathtub-like steel collecting basins was I able to figure out their use.

Steve's woodlot is conveniently located on a steep hillside above his sugar shack so his tapping tubes are assisted by gravity. Even so there was no sap moving. This and the rosy buds of the more advanced red maples confirmed that the syrup season was almost complete.

I realized as we hiked through this pretty copse that I was seeing only part of this operation. Steve would soon have to remove his tubes for washing and sanitizing, repair sections broken by falling trees or gnawed by squirrels, clean out his evaporator and firebox, and thin his woodlot of competing trees. All this work and investment in equipment for a season producing thirty to forty gallons of syrup.

My high regard for Steve himself and farmers in general was again confirmed. Their work can never be valued too highly.

48. PILTDOWN MAN

March 30, 1992

**The hoaxers? A 1915 portrait by John Cooke
of the Piltdown Man sponsors**

With the end of March near at hand, my thoughts turn to April fooling and I recall sadly that hoaxes are not foreign to the study of nature. Perhaps there are some lessons to be learned from recounting what was arguably the greatest of all scientific deceptions.

When I studied biology in high school and college, Piltdown Man was one of what were then commonly referred to as cavemen. These were early examples or even precursors of our own species, identified in each case only by a few bone fragments. The popular press described them as missing links: evolutionary ancestors of man, progeny of apes.

What was exceptional about Piltdown Man was that, unlike the Neanderthals of continental Europe and Java Man of Indonesia, this evidence was found in England.

Early in 1912, Charles Dawson, a practicing English lawyer and amateur geologist and archeologist, showed British Museum paleontologist Arthur Smith Woodward some fragments of a human skull together with a hippopotamus tooth. He had found these artifacts in a gravel pit near the English country town of Piltdown in East Sussex.

Woodward was interested enough to visit the site. A young French colleague, the Jesuit paleontologist, Father Pierre Teilhard, described their ensuing dig: "We were left off on the hunting ground: a grassy strip 4-5 metres wide.... Under this grass, there's a 50-centimetre layer of gravel which is gradually being removed to be used for roads. Armed with picks and sieves, we worked for several hours and finally had success. Dawson discovered a new fragment of the famous human skull; he already had three pieces of it and I myself put a hand on a fragment of an elephant's molar; this made me really worth something in Woodward's eyes. He jumped on the pieces with the enthusiasm of a youth and all the fire that his apparent coldness covered came out."

More evidence followed quickly. Four additional skull pieces were turned up, three on successive days, as Dawson's team shoveled through the gravel. Teeth from another elephant, a mastodon and an extinct beaver were found. More shaped stones appeared.

But the major find was unearthed just weeks later by Dawson and Woodward: a jawbone. This, together with the skull, was to form the evidence for Piltdown Man, not just a new hominid species, but the first identified member of a new genus given the romantic name, Eoanthropus, for "dawn man."

What made the discoverers' announcement to the Geological Society of London so exciting to British archeologists was the fact that the skull, despite its sloping forehead, was clearly human, while the jawbone had characteristics of both man and ape. In particular the teeth showed human grinding patterns while the general configuration of the jaw was clearly apelike.

There were problems of course. The key jaw hinges and canine teeth were missing, but further support came when Father Teilhard conveniently found a canine the following summer.

From the outset there were skeptics. Two Americans, Ales Hrdlicka and Gerrit Miller, argued that the skull and jawbone were from different species, but most anthropologists supported Dawson and Woodward.

It was not until 1949 that the story began to collapse. Fluorine dating proved skull and jawbone to be not 500,000 years old as claimed, but of modern origin. The closer investigation of the evidence that followed showed that the bones and other artifacts were artificially stained, the flint implements worked with a steel knife, the skull spuriously thickened, the molars filed, the fossil animal bones imported and the jawbone that of an orangutan. This was not just a mistake; it was a deliberate and cruel hoax.

The hoaxer has never been established. Although much evidence points to Dawson, many suspects have been named, even including Arthur Conan Doyle, the author of the Sherlock Holmes mysteries.

The more interesting question is why the trickery was so successful. The answers are not comforting. Along with elements of chauvinism and even racism, they include what Steven Jay Gould calls "the influence of strong hope on dubious evidence."

49. MARTHA'S VINEYARD

April 6, 1992

Common Eider

About 20,000 years ago a glacier pushed down over all of New England. It plowed up and pulverized soil and rock, depositing that debris at its southernmost edge in a long east-west hill called a terminal moraine. That hill stretched from where New York City is now located, along Long Island and out through that island's south arm, continuing eastward in a jagged line that passed a few miles south of present Cape Cod.

As this and other huge glaciers retreated, their two mile thick ice masses melted causing ocean levels to rise more than one hundred feet and cover most of the eastern end of this moraine. Today the only hill crests remaining above water in the Massachusetts area are Martha's Vineyard and Nantucket.

My friend Herb Foster and I spent a spring-like day and a half on Martha's Vineyard in mid-March, just before the recent blast of snow and cold moved in from the west. This was my first visit and we could not have picked a better time. The island's population is now about 10,000; in a few weeks it will be ten times that number. Having suffered Cape Cod's summertime miles long traffic jams, I found the Vineyard at this time of year a special delight.

To cross Vineyard Sound we took the 40-minute ferry ride from Wood's Hole to Vineyard Haven. Bracing the icy northeast wind on deck, we were rewarded by seeing a few loons still in their gray and white winter plumage, some red-breasted mergansers, the dapper males as always needing to run a comb through their unruly topknots, and several flights of common eiders. Female eiders look like big chunky black ducks, but males show much white in their head, breast and back. When they fly, they appear white forward, black aft.

We had, of course, too little time. On our first afternoon we spent several hours at the north shore Audubon sanctuary at Felix Neck and the next morning I hiked alone for two hours along the south coast barrier beach leading to Wasque Point on Chappaquiddick. At neither place was there another soul!

These were, of course, very different areas, the sanctuary mostly wooded with beech, red maple, several oaks, sassafras and pitch pine predominant. The trees were only about half the height of the same or similar species in the Buffalo area. There are a number of reasons for this: earlier clear cutting, the poor sandy soil and hurricanes, one of which wreaked havoc on the island just last fall.

Following good New England tradition, residents assign their own unique names. I looked for the tupelo tree, here called beetlebung, and listened for the spring peeper – pinkletink is its delightful local name – but could find neither.

The desolate character of the barrier beach of Norton Point that separates Katama Bay from the open ocean I found equally pleasing. What surprised me was that it shared with Felix Neck an attraction that I had never investigated closely before: seashells.

At Felix Neck seashells had been driven all the way across Sengekontacket Pond from Nantucket Sound to lie high in the bushes back from the water's edge. On the barrier beach they were in the detritus left at high watermark.

Both areas provided rich treasures, everything from tiny bay scallops to channeled whelks, the big curled shells in which you can indeed hear the ocean roar. My favorites were the inch long slipper or boat shells, aptly named because each half shell has an interior shelf like a boat seat or the top of a floppy slipper.

Here too were moon shells, seven inch surf clams and heavy oysters, cast off horseshoe and spider crab shells, a skate's egg case and even a zebra mussel look-alike that turned out to be a small blue mussel.

I know better now the beachcomber's attraction to the seashore.

50. SWANS

April 13, 1992

Tundra Swan

Most western New Yorkers make their annual Easter pilgrimage to the Oak Orchard swamps to see Canada geese. And of course they are richly rewarded. Tens of thousands of these geese stand in pasture stubble or ride high on marsh waters, occasionally rising to the skies to join others in skeins or V's, all the while honking that off-key klaxon.

But some of us, like Warren Button and me, go instead to see white birds: snow geese and tundra or whistling swans. You have to look hard to pick out these geese and even swans from the thousands of mostly gray and black Canadas, but when you find them you are rewarded. When you do locate these white birds, you see not one of an uncountable many but one of a very few.

Each spring the total number of all of these white birds observed in this area may be counted in dozens, sometimes still fewer. This year I was lucky. On April 3, I found 130 tundra swans on Wood Marsh north of Bartel Road in the Tonawanda Wildlife Management Area.

These are majestic birds. They stretch well over four feet long and enjoy a wingspread of seven feet, about the same as that of an eagle. When they sit on the water, their necks rise arrow-straight, giving them a posture that is both regal and graceful. Watching them drifting in stately groups, you realize how right for the finest ballerinas is Tchaikovsky's *Swan Lake*.

Mute Swan

Erect posture is not common to all swans. For years a mute swan wintered in Buffalo Harbor and summered at Tifft Nature Preserve. The neck of this species is usually held in a curved position. (This local swan died a few days ago when it flew into power lines on its five-mile spring migration.)

Even the trumpeter swan, a rarer western species most often seen in Yellowstone Park, generally holds its neck kinked so that it appears to rise out of the forepart of its back. Remarkably one of these birds occurred in the Niagara River a few years ago.

148

Trumpeter Swam with cygnets

The bill of an adult mute swan is also very different: it is largely orange with a black knob where it meets the forehead. Bills of tundra and trumpeter swans are straight and black.

Several years ago I was standing in the yard of my Amherst home when I heard goose-like calling but softer and lower in pitch. I turned just in time to see three tundra swans in perfect echelon pass overhead only a few feet above the trees. They were so close that I could hear the "howf howf howf" of their wing beats.

That was the first time I realized how very fast they fly. Their wing beat is slower than the smaller geese and ducks, giving them the appearance of proportionally slower flight, but in truth their powerful wings are driving them forward at a high rate. One closely monitored migrating group averaged 51 mph on an eleven-hour flight!

Tundra swans need that powerful flight. Those that pass through this region have come from the Chesapeake Bay area. They will continue west from here to North Dakota before they turn north or northwest to fly on to the farthest boundaries of continental North America.

I close these comments about tundra swans by recounting one of the saddest events in local ornithological history. On March 15, 1908, 102 of these beautiful birds, evidently blinded by a severe rainstorm, were caught in the rapids above Niagara Falls and swept over. James Savage reported, "These splendid birds, helpless after their terrible plunge over the cataract, were dashed against the ice bridge by the swift current, amid cakes of loose ice. Some had been killed outright by the falls. Others...were soon imprisoned in the ice where their pitiful cries were heartrending.... It was not long before men and boys, armed with guns and sticks, became the chief factors in the closing scene."

51. FROG SONGS

April 20,1992

Green Frog
Karen Lee Lewis photo

It all started on a rare warm day recently when I was hiking south of the village of Dalton. From a marsh just ahead came a quacking noise like several small ducks gossiping in low tones. When I approached, I could see that the water area was small, perhaps ten yards square. But no matter how hard I looked, I could find no source for the sound. Even though the quacking continued, there were certainly no ducks in that small pond.

I stepped forward carefully until the sound came from almost underfoot. It was very difficult to describe. The notes I recorded at the time read, "Low pitched, guttural chattering."

My approach didn't bother the caller, but it stopped promptly when a harrier came patrolling from the other side of the swamp.

By this time I had, of course, decided that I had been listening to a frog whose voice was unfamiliar. That wasn't unusual because I knew the calls of only two amphibians. One of those came to me now from the back of this same pool. It was the lovely single note of the spring peeper, a stretched out "peeeeep" that is slightly accented at the end.

The other I will not hear until hot nights in July when bullfrogs will strum "jug-o'-rum" on their bass viols.

But intrigued now by this strange sound, on the spot I assigned myself some homework: learn the calls of our local frogs.

I had purchased what I needed for this task from the Buffalo Museum last fall. It is a record entitled, "Voices of the Night." I had set it aside — it was too late in the year to be useful at the time — and almost forgotten it. Now my wife found the record and played it for me.

Frog after frog, toad after toad ribbitted, croaked, trilled, and even barked, but it was not until well into the second side of the record that I heard the familiar quacking. The narrator identified it as a wood frog.

Just two days later on a birding excursion in the Iroquois National Wildlife Refuge, I was able to point out to my companions the call of another wood frog. Doing so I felt just as pumped up as my sixth grade daughter must have when she proudly asked at the dinner table, "Please pass the sodium chloride."

There are ten local frogs and toads among the 36 on this record. Here are my notes on the other seven. Many are already busy calling at this time of year making our marshlands very noisy places.

The Western chorus frog is the very common amphibian whose noisy creaking sounds like a fingernail run along a comb. Whole groups of them join in this monotonous chorus day and night. The sound is nonetheless quite refreshing after the long silence of winter.

The gray treefrog is a relative of the spring peeper. Its call is an open, liquid, single note trill of a second or two duration. It will begin to sing in mid-May.

The American toad's song is a high, 6 to 30-second, steady trill, almost a buzz. When a second toad chimes in, it always does so at a slightly different pitch in order, I assume, to differentiate its personal notes. The strange call of the related Fowler's toad is a short harsh "scraaaaah." The range of Fowler's toad doesn't include western New York but it extends in Canada to the Niagara River and in

Pennsylvania to Lake Erie. Thus you should listen for it in those locations.

Leopard Frog
Karen Lee Lewis photo

The pickerel frog simply snores and the notes of its relative, the Northern leopard frog, are so unmusical that they sound to me like knocking and scratching. No wonder: they are often pronounced underwater.

Finally, the green frog's call is a series of explosive banjo twangs. It will perform from June to mid-August.

Join me in listening for these spring and summer voices of the night.

52. BROWNS AND GREENS

April 27, 1992

Wild Turkeys

When the temperature rises and the snow retreats even from the high country of the Southern Tier, we enter what I call the brown season. An artist's palette for March and April in the countryside would seem to require only the somber shades of this drab hue.

As I walk now through a ridge woodlot just north of the Livingston County village of Swain, my eyes register only this color. Brown leaves cover the ground, all of their yellow and red pigments long ago leached into the soil. A few leaves of oak and beech retain their last hold on parent trees, but they too are brown: the oak dark, the beech remarkably light and translucent. Dead logs add additional shades. Underfoot my boots push aside the humus and uncover the still darker brown mud below. The two birds I flush, a grouse and a turkey, contribute their browns as well. The dreary rainy day dulls even these colors and all around me tree trunks, branches and twigs stitch still more brown into this enveloping dismal tapestry.

But even in this somber landscape, when I begin to look more carefully, I find a brighter color. It is green. This is, of course, the color that will take over by mid-May, but it is here now and has been here through the long winter in what sociologists might call "reduced circumstances."

Among the profligate colors of May and June these greens will be lost, but now their quality is enhanced by the drab background. A few weeks ago they provided rich contrast with the stark white of snow; now they do so against those browns.

Conifers contribute most of these greens. At each stream crossing, I find a small grove of hemlocks, their tiny needles forming filigrees around the brown-gray branches. In drier areas there are pines, here both red and white, as well as Norway spruce. Some of these trees are topped with lighter hued candles of new growth.

Lower down there is green as well. Two ferns remain green all year: the Christmas fern and the woodfern or shield fern. They are in marked contrast. The Christmas fern is deep green at this time of year, the woodfern much lighter. Each frond of the woodfern is made up of tiny replicas called pinnas and each of these in turn has smaller leaf-like structures called pinnules. These replications are called cuts, so these ferns are twice cut. The fronds of the Christmas fern are only singly cut. Each pinna is oddly lopsided, which makes it reminiscent of those big stockings hung from the mantle at Christmastime. Its common name derives from this association.

Also hugging the forest floor are several species of clubmoss. These include the rich green ground pine and running cedar, each a tiny miniature of the tree that shares its name. They will, however, never grow any larger than their current six-inch height.

Along one shielded creek bank I also find an extensive growth of partridgeberry with its trailing vine-like stems and round glossy green leaves. There is even a single red berry that the grouse and mice have not yet found.

Finally, mosses cling to damp rocks and tree stumps, some thinly plastered to their surface, some growing thickly like a rich lawn. Their color varies from deep green to a light shade, almost lime.

All of these are evergreens. But on this hike I find three other greens: greens that are harbingers of the spring that will finally come. Here are a few vanguard leeks. And here two isolated leaf blades thrust up through the duff. One, brown stained, will grow into a trout lily. The other, daintily laced, will one day sport Dutchman's breeches.

Not everything is brown after all.

Author

Gerald R. Rising Sr., the Gerry Rising of these columns, is State University of New York Distinguished Teaching Professor Emeritus at the University at Buffalo. His "day job" at the university was working with school mathematics teachers and teaching mathematics and computer science. Rising is the author of over a dozen mathematics texts, the most recent *About Mathematics*, written for college liberal arts students, as well as several hundred journal articles about mathematics.

Not a professional biologist, Professor Rising seeks to communicate to his readers his own love of nature.

Professor Rising lives with his wife Doris in Amherst, New York, a Buffalo suburb. He has two children, four grandchildren and a great granddaughter.

Photographer

Harold Stiver is a partner in a financial services company who lives with his wife Elaine in Paris, Ontario. He has two daughters and one grandson whom he spoils relentlessly.

He has long had a fascination with the natural world and has traveled widely exploring and photographing it. You can see more of his images at http://www.singularvideo.com.

He is the author of a series of eBook Guides for Photographers and Explorers covering subjects like Waterfalls, Old Mills and Covered Bridges. They are available at Amazon and other popular distributors.